BRITISH GEOLOGICAL SURVEY
Natural Environment Research Council

British Regional Geology

North Wales

THIRD EDITION

By Bernard Smith, MA, ScD, FRS,
and T. Neville George, DSc, PhD

Completely revised by T. Neville
George, DSc, PhD, DèsSc
(Professor of Geology in the
University of Glasgow)

LONDON   HER MAJESTY'S STATIONERY OFFICE   1961

HER MAJESTY'S STATIONERY OFFICE

HMSO publications are available from:

HMSO Publications Centre
(Mail and telephone orders)
PO Box 276, London SW8 5DT
Telephone orders (01) 622 3316
General enquiries (01) 211 5656
*Queueing system in operation for both
numbers*

HMSO Bookshops
49 High Holborn, London WC1V 6HB
(01) 211 5656 (Counter service only)
258 Broad Street, Birmingham B1 2HE
(021) 643 3740
Southey House, 33 Wine Street, Bristol
BS1 2BQ   (0272) 264306
9 Princess Street, Manchester M60 8AS
(061) 834 7201
80 Chichester Street, Belfast BT1 4JY
(0232) 238451
71 Lothian Road, Edinburgh
EH3 9AZ   (031) 228 4181

HMSO's Accredited Agents
(see Yellow Pages)

And through good booksellers

BRITISH GEOLOGICAL SURVEY

Keyworth, Nottinghamshire NG12 5GG
Plumtree (060 77) 6111

Murchison House, West Mains Road,
Edinburgh EH9 3LA   (031) 667 1000

The full range of Survey publications is
available through the Sales Desks at Keyworth and Murchison House. Selected
items are stocked by the Geological
Museum Bookshop, Exhibition Road,
London SW7 2DE; all other items may be
obtained through the BGS London
Information Office in the Geological
Museum ((01) 589 4090). All the books
are listed in HMSO's Sectional List 45.

*The British Geological Survey carries out
the geological survey of Great Britain and
Northern Ireland (the latter as an agency
service for the government of Northern
Ireland), and of the surrounding
continental shelf, as well as its basic
research projects. It also undertakes
programmes of British technical aid in
geology in developing countries as
arranged by the Overseas Development
Administration.*

*The British Geological Survey is a
component body of the Natural
Environment Research Council.*

FOREWORD TO THE THIRD EDITION

Further revision of this work has been found necessary and desirable for a third edition
and this has again been undertaken by Prof. T. Neville George. Much of the text has been
rewritten, numerous new text-figures have been introduced and modifications made to
some of the original illustrations, including the plates.

C. J. Stubblefield
Director

Geological Survey and Museum
Exhibition Road
South Kensington
London SW7

23rd January 1961

First published 1935
Third edition 1961
Seventh impression 1987

ISBN 0 11 880145 7

*Maps and diagrams in this book use
topography based on Ordnance Survey
mapping*

CONTENTS

ILLUSTRATIONS

FIGURES IN TEXT

v

PLATES

*The numbers in brackets are those of the corresponding Geological
Survey photographs, copies of which may be obtained on application.*

Llyn Llydaw and Snowdon summit (Yr Wyddfa)

(A. 6491)

Plate I

NORTH WALES

I. INTRODUCTION

BOUNDARIES AND PHYSICAL FEATURES

NORTH WALES is only imperfectly defined by physical features. It has natural boundaries along the north and west coasts and along the eastern hills bordering the Cheshire plain; but southwards it merges without sharp distinction into the highlands of Central Wales and south-eastwards into the hills of Shropshire. For convenience, it is considered to be bounded on the east by an arbitrary line running from Chester by Ellesmere to Welshpool, and thence by the Severn valley to Newtown; on the south the line continues from Newtown to Machynlleth and the Dyfi estuary (see Pl. XII).

Most of the major rivers bear little obvious relationship to the geological structures of the rocks beneath (upon which they appear to have been superimposed), so that the area is not readily subdivided into provinces according to the arrangement of the drainage systems. On the other hand, there is a broad concordance of topography and rock-type, and a geological subdivision of the area tends to delineate the mountainous from the low-lying tracts. Thus the rugged, precipitous mountain mass of Snowdonia, extending at lower altitudes into the Lleyn peninsula, coincides with a downfold of Ordovician rocks compressed between two upfolded belts of older rocks—the Pre-Cambrian and Cambrian rocks of the Bangor–Llanberis–Caernarvon country to the north, and the Cambrian rocks of the northern flanks of the Harlech Dome to the south. The Ordovician rocks of Snowdonia and Lleyn (Pls. VII and VIII) are in large part igneous in origin and relatively resistant to denudation, and form the highest ground: Yr Wyddfa, the central peak of Snowdon at 3560 ft, is the highest mountain in southern Britain. Swinging southwards as a half-circle around the Harlech Dome, the similar mountains of the Moelwyns, the Arenigs, the Arans, and Cader Idris (Pl. VI) are carved out of similar Ordovician lavas and ashes: they are eroded into great terraced escarpments facing towards the centre of the Dome, and form with Snowdonia the most imposing elements of the Welsh landscape. In turn they are bounded to the east and south by extensive tracts of dissected plateau—an area of gentle undulations with few mountain peaks, underlain by the soft sediments of the Upper Ordovician and Silurian beds of the Central Wales syncline, and reaching its highest point in Plynlimon. Within the Harlech Dome, the tough grits and flags of the Cambrian sediments form high and rough country (Pl. III), though it fails to equal in grandeur the crags and peaks of Snowdonia.

The Berwyn Hills (Pl. VB) are carved from an independent group of Ordovician strata forming a dome with a general east-and-west trend. They have gentler outlines than the heights of Snowdonia or of Cader Idris and the Arenigs, for the thicknesses of volcanic rocks they contain are small when contrasted with the huge piles of the western mountains.

The north-eastern tracts of North Wales are composed partly of Silurian sediments, partly of the Carboniferous rocks of the Flintshire and Denbighshire

1

coalfields and their borders. Silurian grits and shales form the Denbighshire Moors, a monotonous area of heathy plateau, deeply dissected by rivers, and cleft by the down-faulted rift of the Vale of Clwyd which isolates the Clwydian Range. Both scenically and geologically the moorlands are very similar to the plateau of Central Wales in the neighbourhood of Plynlimon. The erosion of the gently dipping Carboniferous rocks, particularly of the beds of limestone and sandstone in the lower part, has produced a very different type of scenery: the strata are gently inclined towards the east along an outcrop extending from Prestatyn to Oswestry, and give rise along their western margins to typical scarp-and-dip features, of which the Eglwyseg escarpment near Llangollen (Pl. VIIIA) is one of the most prominent. Eastwards, successively younger Carboniferous rocks appear and descend with milder contours to the Cheshire and Shropshire plains where they become buried under a blanket of soft New Red Sandstone that continues for many miles into the English Midlands.

Along much of the coast the general correspondence of the surface features with the geological structure is not apparent, for comparatively recent emergence of the area has exposed a landscape dominated by plains, mainly the product of marine erosion, of very subdued relief. This surface cuts across beds regardless of their age, of their relative hardness, and of the degree of folding, faulting, and metamorphism they have suffered. It is best seen as the Menaian Platform of Anglesey, where it is underlain by intensely hardened and altered Pre-Cambrian gneisses and schists, by soft, easily eroded but sharply folded Ordovician and Silurian shales, and by gently dipping Carboniferous limestones and sandstones. It is also well displayed as wave-cut platforms, elevated to still higher levels, on the mainland of Caernarvonshire (Pl. VIIIB) where it abuts against ancient cliffs that now form the fronts of the Snowdonian mountains. Many of the monadnock hills of Lleyn similarly stand up as ' islands ' above the fringing uplifted platform.

Most of the minor and some of the major elements of the scenery are attributable to the work of ice during the Glacial period, ice which on its final disappearance left behind varied and extensive deposits of boulder clay and other morainic detritus, and which in its movement carved and moulded the rocks, shattered and bevelled hillsides, trenched and gouged valleys, excavated cirques, and diverted river systems.

GEOLOGICAL SUCCESSION

North Wales, apart from the northern and north-eastern fringes, is essentially a region of Lower Palaeozoic rocks, displaying as a whole one of the thickest and most complete sequences of Cambrian, Ordovician, and Silurian strata to be found in Europe. Of the remaining formations, the underlying Pre-Cambrian is well displayed in Anglesey, and in smaller outcrops on the mainland of Caernarvonshire; and the Carboniferous and New Red Sandstone cover extensive tracts on the borders. In contrast, Mesozoic and Tertiary marine sediments are wholly absent. The full sequence is as follows (see also Pl. XII):

GEOLOGICAL SEQUENCE

VI. RECENT: alluvium, blown sands, and other superficial deposits, and slightly older coastal submerged peats and clays.

V. PLEISTOCENE: widespread morainic boulder clay, silts, sands and gravels of the Glacial period.

IV. TERTIARY: represented by minor igneous intrusions (dykes) only.

III. MESOZOIC: Triassic New Red Sandstone in the Vale of Clwyd and in the Cheshire and Shropshire plains; Jurassic and Cretaceous rocks absent.

II. PALAEOZOIC: represented by the following systems, in downward succession:
    (5) Carboniferous: in and bordering the Flint and Denbigh coalfields, in the Vale of Clwyd, and in Anglesey.
    (4) Old Red Sandstone: in Anglesey only.
    (3) Silurian: in the Denbighshire Moors, the Clwydian Range, and the northern extension of the Central Wales syncline between the Harlech Dome and the Berwyn anticline.
    (2) Ordovician: in Snowdonia, the Lleyn peninsula, the Moelwyns, the Arenigs, the Arans, Cader Idris, the tract between Machynlleth and Bala, the Berwyn Hills, and much of Anglesey.
    (1) Cambrian: in the Harlech Dome, the Bethesda–Llanberis–Nantlle district, and St. Tudwal's Peninsula.

I. PRE-CAMBRIAN: in Anglesey (the Mona Complex), south-western Lleyn, a ridge extending from Bangor to Caernarvon, and a second parallel ridge running from near Bethesda through Cwmyglo and Penygroes to the coast of Caernarvon Bay.

The accompanying section (Fig. 1) diagrammatically illustrates the occurrence of the various systems in North Wales.

HISTORY OF GEOLOGICAL RESEARCH

Systematic geological research in North Wales commenced in the early part of the nineteenth century, although incidental observations had been made from time to time by such early writers as Giraldus Cambrensis, Leyland, and Pennant, mainly in reference to agriculture and mining.

Four stages in formal research may be recognized: an early stage in which surveys were sporadic and local; a second stage in which a comprehensive attempt was made to unravel the regional stratigraphy and structure (mainly by Adam Sedgwick); a third stage in which detailed mapping was carried out by the Geological Survey; and a fourth stage, continuing to the present time, in which attention has been mainly concentrated on particular problems of current interest.

William Smith did not confine his attention to the Secondary rocks of England. He appears to have visited North Wales, and in his geological map of 1815 referred nearly all the rocks of the north and west of Wales to ' Killas ' and ' Slate ', though he regarded as igneous rock the Coedana granite of Anglesey. Greenough's map of England and Wales, published in 1820, was essentially a compilation based on Smith's map, with additional records notably of outcrops of igneous rock (' greenstone ').

In 1831 Adam Sedgwick and R. I. Murchison commenced work in Wales. Sedgwick, who had already gained experience in the Lake District, boldly set about the task of disentangling the structure of the mountain district of Snowdonia and Lleyn, where he found a thick development of deformed rocks of which neither top nor bottom was then known. He set to work with such purpose that before his first season was over he had made an outline geological map of the whole of Caernarvonshire. The following year (1832) he returned and undertook the most severe task of his geological life, the interpretation and partial delineation of the order and principal flexures of all the older deposits of Merioneth, Montgomeryshire, and Denbighshire. He made further traverses and revisions in 1834, 1842–1843, and 1846. In 1842–43 he was accompanied by J. W. Salter, who joined the Geological Survey in 1846, and who, with

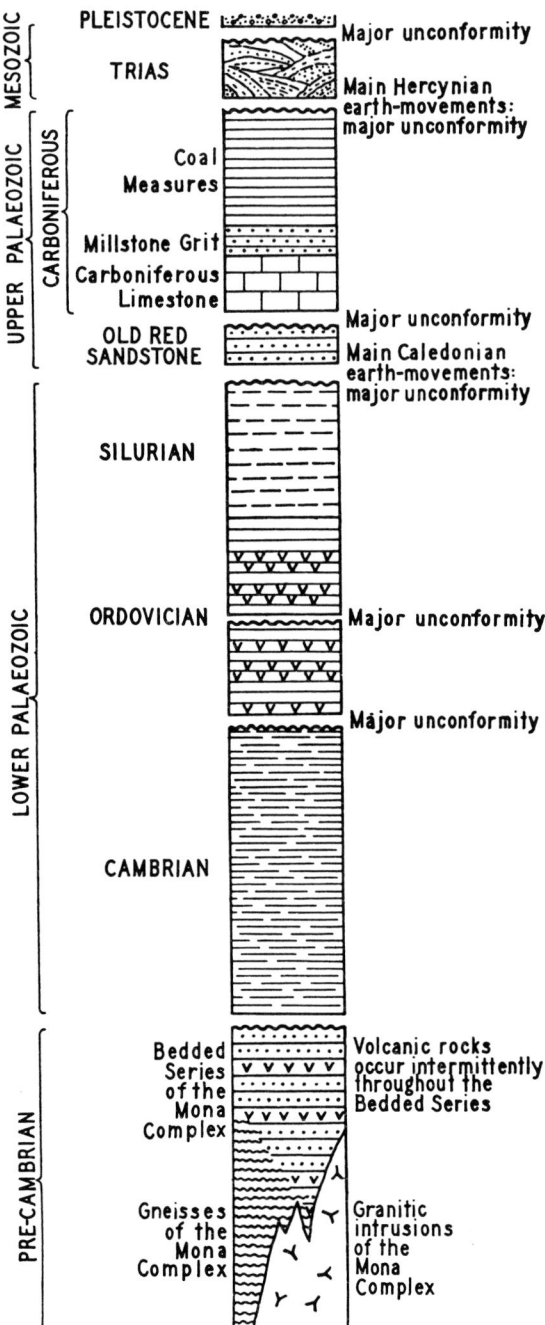

FIG. 1: *The rock succession in North Wales*

The thicknesses of the Pre-Cambrian rocks are not to scale; the rest of the section is on a scale of approximately 1 inch to 10,000 feet.

J. de C. Sowerby, drew up his fossil lists. Sedgwick's map of North Wales, on the scale of 1 in. to 8 miles, appeared in 1845, and was accompanied by illustrative geological sections.

In 1835 Sedgwick termed his beds ' Cambrian,' and divided them into Upper, Middle, and Lower. Murchison, working westwards from the Welsh border-land, divided his rocks into Upper and Lower Silurian, and (as then supposed) unfossiliferous Cambrian. With advancing knowledge it became evident that Sedgwick's Upper and Middle Cambrian were in great part the equivalents of Murchison's Lower Silurian and there was prolonged dispute between the two authors partly on the geological facts but mainly on the significance of the stratigraphical terms each applied to the rock formations. In 1879, after thirty years of disagreement, most of the controversial beds were, on Charles Lapworth's proposal, classed as the Ordovician system—a middle division of the Lower Palaeozoic between the Silurian and Cambrian systems of to-day. In Geological Survey usage, however, in deference to Murchison, the Ordovician rocks continued to be termed Lower Silurian until the beginning of the 20th century.

Daniel Sharpe's map of North Wales on the scale of 1 in. to 5½ miles appeared a year later than Sedgwick's: in it the main outline of the geological structure, as now understood, was shown clearly for the first time.

During the third period the systematic survey of North Wales was com-menced (in 1846) by the Geological Survey under Sir Henry De la Beche. Upon this survey A. C. Ramsay, W. T. Aveline, A. R. C. Selwyn, and J. B. Jukes were engaged, with J. W. Salter as palaeontologist. The whole area, including Anglesey, was mapped by 1852 on the 1-in. scale. Between 1853 and 1857 Ramsay and his colleagues revised several sheets in Caernarvonshire, Merioneth, and Denbighshire, and in 1858 a geological map of Wales and adjacent districts, on the scale of 4 miles to 1 in. was issued by the Survey. This was revised in 1879. An important feature of the Survey's work was the con-struction of a series of beautifully executed horizontal sections, the profiles for which were made in the field with theodolite and chain, displaying in detail the geology of some of the wildest parts of the country on the scale of 6 in. to 1 mile.

In this period, Belt, building on the palaeontological work of Salter, William-son, and others, described the sequence of fossils in the Upper Cambrian rocks.

Sedgwick, working practically single-handed and under extremely difficult conditions, was an outstanding pioneer; but Ramsay and his colleagues gave the first comprehensive account of the geology of North Wales as a whole. Their work is notable not only for the manner in which the complicated structure was analysed and mapped; not only for the ability shown in separating the rocks of igneous origin from one another and from flanking sediments; but also for the memoir in which the geology was described and illustrated, and, when the second edition was written in 1881, for the stimulating manner in which the evolution of landscape was discussed. Ramsay also led the way to a closer understanding of the work of ice in Britain, and in his *Old Glaciers of Switzerland and North Wales* (1860) put forward the first convincing argument for the place of glacial erosion in moulding the Welsh landscape.

The fourth period, spanning the last half-century, has been marked by increasing attention to detail on the part of both official and other geologists. Six-inch maps being available, a large-scale revision of parts of Flintshire and Denbighshire was made by the Survey in 1884-1886, and the whole of the

Flintshire and Denbighshire coalfields as well as adjoining areas of Lower Carboniferous and Lower Palaeozoic rocks were re-mapped between 1910 and 1919.

Of the local studies by individual geologists, special mention should be made of Harker's essay on the Bala Volcanic Series of Caernarvonshire, and of the researches of Lapworth, Elles and Wood on the Ordovician and Silurian graptolite faunas which laid the detailed foundations for accurate zoning.

In Anglesey the special problems presented by the highly contorted Pre-Cambrian rocks were first comprehensively attacked by Greenly who during a quarter-century (1895–1919) mapped the island on the 6-in. (parts on the 25-in.) scale, and wrote the official memoir.

The author wishes to thank Dr. C. J. Stubblefield for helpful criticism and suggestions, and for supervising the preparation of the text-figures of fossils.

II. PRE-CAMBRIAN ROCKS

ANGLESEY AND LLEYN

THE MOST EXTENSIVE tract of Pre-Cambrian rocks, the Mona Complex of Anglesey (Fig. 2), has been described in great detail by Greenly, who applied to his study of the area the methods of mapping established and developed in the Pre-Cambrian country of the Scottish Highlands by Clough, Peach, and Horne. Similar rocks occur in Lleyn, between Nevin and Bardsey Island, where they have been described by Matley. The Complex comprises a series, or several

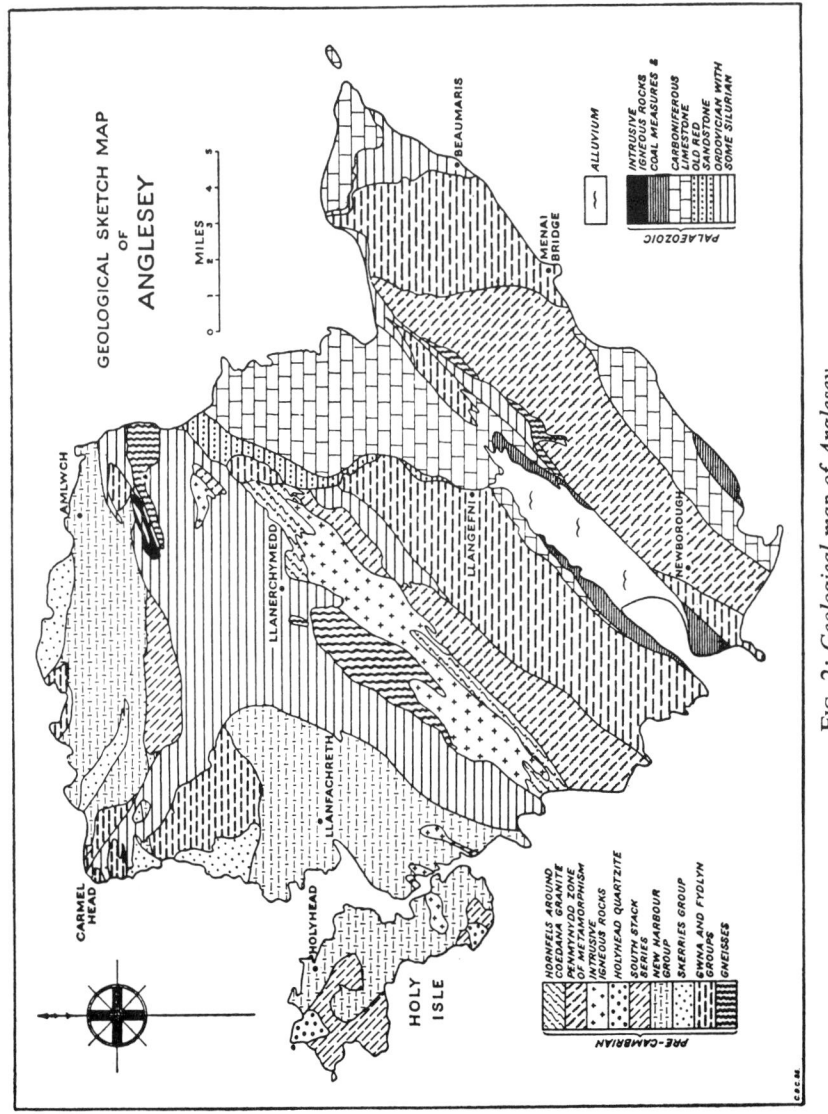

FIG. 2: Geological map of Anglesey

series, of highly altered rocks, which may be divided into three broad groups of rock-types, and which have been intricately folded and deformed by intense pressures that resulted from powerful earth-movements. There is little doubt that the rocks are older than the Cambrian sediments of North Wales, for although no beds of proved Cambrian age rest directly upon them, the profound degree of metamorphism they have suffered is far greater than that exhibited by any of the neighbouring Palaeozoic rocks of the mainland, including the Cambrian strata of the Nantlle–Bethesda slate belt and the underlying Padarn Volcanic Series. Moreover, they are directly overlain by Ordovician sediments with great discordance, and as the Ordovician follows in unconformable sequence above the Cambrian on the mainland, it is reasonable to suppose that Cambrian rocks were formerly present in Anglesey but are now absent only because they suffered erosion at the beginning of Ordovician times.

Three main rock-groups—the Gneisses, the Bedded Series, and the Coedana granite (and similar intrusions)—were recognised by Greenly, who thought them to have been formed during three successive and distinct periods. He regarded the Gneisses as a foundation group, an old floor, upon which the much younger Bedded Series was deposited unconformably, both groups being later intruded by the granites. Shackleton has argued, however, that Greenly was misled in his criteria both of age and of structure in thinking the gneisses to be the oldest group; and he has presented strong evidence, especially in Lleyn, that they may well be no more than highly metamorphosed representatives of the Bedded Series, which are thus probably the oldest known rocks of North Wales.

The Bedded Series. In a thickness of the order of 20,000 ft, the Bedded Series appears to have been deposited in a large crustal down-warp, a geosyncline of magnitude comparable with the later Lower Palaeozoic geosyncline. The trend of the down-warp and the positions of its margins are wholly unknown since the small outcrops of the rocks, which are limited to Anglesey and Lleyn, do not display sufficiently clear lateral variations in rock-type to allow reconstruction of the contemporary geography.

The rocks are typical geosynclinal sediments—grits, greywackes, and conglomerates, shales and muds. In the long period of their accumulation volcanoes were active on at least four major occasions, lavas, ashes, and tuffs being found interbedded with the marine sediments. On lithological differences Greenly was able to recognise six major divisions of the series, which he placed in the following descending succession:

(6) Holyhead Quartzite: a white very pure recrystallized sandstone, containing in the lower part less pure rocks like those of the South Stack Series.

(5) South Stack Series: a mixed sequence of grits, greywackes, and sandstones with interbedded shales, some of the sediments showing graded bedding. (See Pl. IIB).

(4) New Harbour Group: alternating fine grits, flags, quartzites, and shales, with beds of jasper and a thick development of spilitic pillow-lavas.

(3) Skerries Group: grey and green massive grits, containing much fragmental volcanic debris, some of them being dominantly pyroclastic dusts and ashes. The Gwyddel Beds may be the equivalent rocks in Lleyn.

(2) Gwna Group: a varied sequence of grits, shales and some limestones, interbedded with sodic spilitic lavas and tuffs, and beds of jasper. Some of the spilites show well developed pillow structure (Pl. IIA). Many of the limestones are oolitic or coarsely pisolitic.

(1) Fydlyn Group: soda-rich highly acid lavas ('felsites'), with interbedded layers of pyroclastic tuffs and dusts.

(A.1211)

A. Pillow lavas of the Gwna Group, Newborough Warren

Plate II

B. Major folding in the Mona Complex, South Stack, Holy Isle

(A.1261)

The rocks are so much deformed that the sequence cannot be read by direct observation and Greenly was compelled to fall back on indirect means to determine relative age. He thought he could identify derived pebbles of Gwna jasper in the South Stack Series, and therefore placed the Fydlyn Group at the base of the succession. As a corollary, to explain the apparently inverted sequence at a number of localities, he postulated the occurrence of large-scale overfolds and nappes like the structures found in the Scottish Highlands. The evidence of depositional order to be seen in graded and rhythmic bedding, however, and of the true attitude of the folds as shown by directions of fold-axes in the smaller anticlines and synclines, appears to contradict the inferences (notoriously deceptive in such altered rocks) got from derived fragments; for jaspers like those utilised by Greenly are repeatedly found in the Bedded Series and may well occur in older members of the group at horizons not now exposed, or they may have been derived from still older formations. Shackleton has therefore argued that Greenly may have been mistaken, and that the evidence favours, and is more simply interpreted by, an inference that Greenly's sequence in the Bedded Series should be reversed, the Holyhead Quartzite being the oldest member, the Fydlyn Group the youngest.

Structure. Much of the difficulty in interpreting the stratigraphical sequence in the Bedded Series derives from the acute deformation and metamorphism the rocks have suffered. Greenly showed that in Pre-Cambrian times orogenic (mountain-building) earth-movements of great intensity compressed the strata into immense anticlines and synclines: he thought the largest folds were of the order of miles in wave-length, and that they collapsed along their crests to form overfolds, sometimes becoming recumbent. These enormous structures were in their turn buckled into secondary folds of large dimensions (Fig. 3), a few of which are directly visible as folds (for example, near the South Stack at Holyhead, where they sweep up and down more than 400 ft of cliff-face; see Pl. IIB). The major secondary folds were in their turn corrugated into innumerable minor folds, visible in most exposures on the island, while yet again these were plicated into minimum folds, often sheared to show strain-slip cleavage. Like the larger folds, the lesser plications commonly collapsed and were replaced by thrusts, which in some places are so numerous as to destroy the original structures of the rock, tearing it into a mass of lenticular strips.

At sufficient depths below the surface the orogenic stresses did not lead to the development of great folds but altered the rocks in a more profound fashion. Becoming in some degree plastic, the sediments collapsed internally to form foliated and banded schists, their constituent minerals being transformed both physically and chemically. The members of the Bedded Series in present outcrops are thus seen to pass laterally, where they are sufficiently metamorphosed, into rocks that have more or less completely lost their original detrital texture and constituents and are now mica-chlorite-hornblende schists, in which there is often a development of the blue sodium-hornblende glaucophane. The most strongly schistose rocks were distinguished by Greenly as belonging to the Penmynydd Zone of metamorphism. These long-recognised changes have led Shackleton to the conclusion, supported by evidence of lateral passage in Lleyn, that the Gneisses similarly are not an independent and more ancient rock-group but are the product of still greater alteration of members of the Bedded Series.

The Gneisses. Because of their complete loss of primary characters, Greenly looked upon the Gneisses as the oldest rocks of Anglesey; and he thought they could be placed in a structural position unconformably beneath the Bedded

Series. If however the sequence that Greenly deduced in the Bedded Series is in fact inverted, some of the Gneisses appear structurally to lie above the

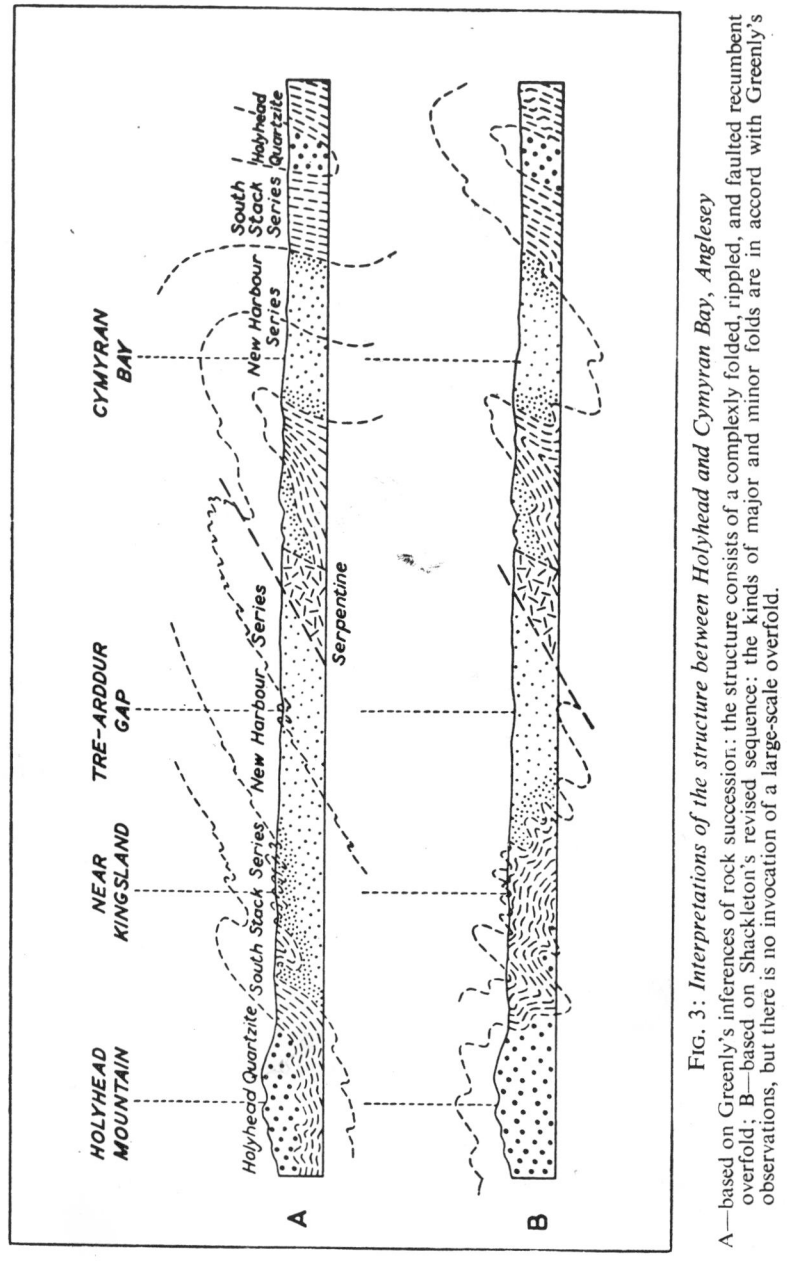

FIG. 3: *Interpretations of the structure between Holyhead and Cymyran Bay, Anglesey*

A—based on Greenly's inferences of rock succession: the structure consists of a complexly folded, rippled, and faulted recumbent overfold; B—based on Shackleton's revised sequence: the kinds of major and minor folds are in accord with Greenly's observations, but there is no invocation of a large-scale overfold.

horizon of the Holyhead Quartzite. In places they contain members that lithologically are scarcely to be distinguished from rocks of the Penmynydd Zone; and the group as a whole carries to an extreme the graded changes seen in progressive development in the sediments and the schists.

Lithologically the gneisses are roughly banded and foliated rocks of coarse grain. Sometimes they are light-coloured and 'acidic', sometimes dark and 'gabbroic'.

In Lleyn, where the greater part of the Bedded Series is referred to the Gwna Group and the sequence includes spilitic pillow-lavas (strikingly displayed near Porth Dinlleyn and Aberdaron) and lenticles of jasper and limestone, the finer beds are metamorphosed to phyllites (the Aber Geirch Phyllites) or to mica-chlorite schists. They may be seen, with increasing grade of metamorphism, to merge into gneisses without any recognisable unconformity, the gneisses being streakily banded by the introduction of granitic material. Such rocks, combining primary sedimentary features with secondary 'intrusive' features, are mixed rocks, migmatites, and in their turn provide a link with the third main rock-group of the Mona Complex recognised by Greenly—the intrusions.

The Igneous Intrusions. The Coedana granite is the largest of the igneous intrusions. It is a coarse-textured rock sometimes containing felspar crystals over an inch in length, but in places the matrix is finer-grained and the rock passes into a felspar-porphyry. The Sarn granite of Lleyn is similar in lithology. With the dominant acidic rocks there occur dioritic and gabbroic intrusions both in Anglesey and in Lleyn, some becoming ultrabasic serpentines.

Greenly recognised that the igneous rocks were injected at a late stage in the folding and metamorphism of the sediments of the Bedded Series, and regarded the movements and the injection as directly associated. Shackleton has completed the theoretical synthesis by introducing an intermediate stage of gneiss-formation, his sequence of events being geosynclinal deposition of the Bedded Series, deformation by crustal pressure, metamorphic change to schists, local recrystallization with conversion to migmatitic gneisses by 'granitization' or 'permeation' at a late stage of the orogenic movements, and finally intrusion of the transgressive granitic masses through sediments, schists, and gneisses.

Where the large intrusions (notably the Coedana granite) are found in contact with some of the finer sediments they are seen to have baked the country rock to a splintery hornfels in an aureole of thermal metamorphism (See Fig. 2. In Pl. XII the hornfels is not distinguished from the associated igneous rocks).

The 'Mélange'. A peculiar rock-type occurring in parts of the Mona Complex is composed of a tumbled mass of fragments, angular and ill-sorted, some many yards across, others microscopic, that lie in a green schistose matrix. The fragments are of phyllite, schist, greywacke, quartzite, limestone, pillow-lava, and other rocks, derived from a variety of sources. This 'mélange', several hundred feet thick, crops out over many square miles in Anglesey and reappears in Lleyn; Bardsey Island is virtually composed of it. In accordance with his theories of over-folding and thrusting, Greenly supposed the Mélange to be a gigantic fault breccia, a product of tectonic friction developed along the sole of a nappe. Shackleton has suggested, however, that, although it is indirectly due to and contemporaneous with the main orogenic movements, it is a primary rock-type and is better regarded as a subaerial landslip deposit formed in gravitational avalanches of fragments of poorly-coherent rocks, that tumbled down the steepening flanks of the more acute folds or upthrust masses.

THE BANGOR AND PADARN RIDGES

Elsewhere on the mainland of North Wales Pre-Cambrian rocks are exposed only in two narrow parallel ridges (Fig. 4), the one extending from Bangor to

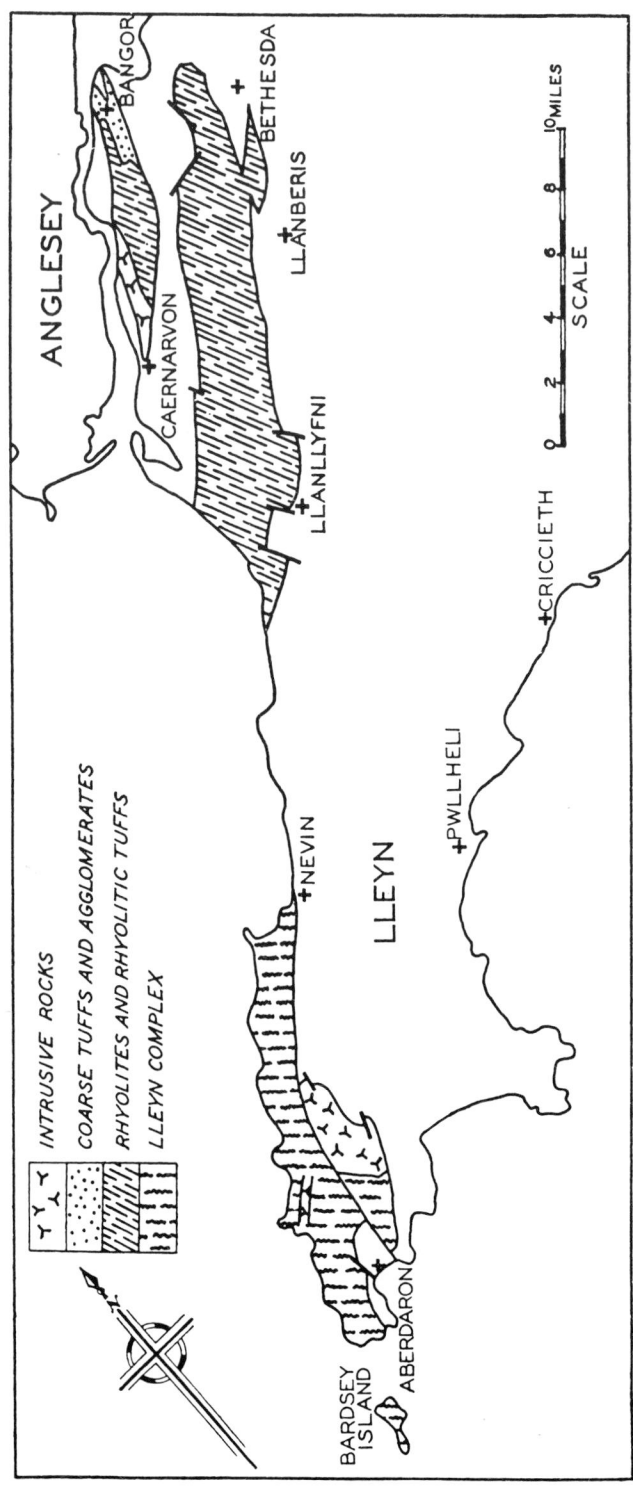

FIG. 4: *Outline map showing the distribution of Pre-Cambrian rocks on the mainland of North Wales*

Caernarvon (the Bangor ridge), the other from near Bethesda to Penygroes (the Padarn ridge). They differ greatly from the highly metamorphosed rocks of Anglesey and Lleyn, and cannot be correlated with them; their low degree of alteration may indicate that they are not everywhere of Pre-Cambrian age; they certainly were formed at a time long after the rocks of the Mona Complex.

The coastal ridge, from Bangor to Caernarvon, consists of a group of igneous rocks collectively known as the Bangor Volcanic Series (Greenly's Arvonian Series). Although largely comprising acid rhyolitic lavas and quartz-felsites, with tuffs, agglomerates, breccias, and grits, it also includes at the south-western end of the ridge the coarse aplitic granite of Twt Hill.

The Padarn ridge is free from contemporaneous intrusions, and consists of acid and sub-acid (rhyolitic and andesitic) lavas, with occasional tuffs and agglomerates; together they comprise the Clogwyn (or Padarn) Volcanic Group, and are certainly of Pre-Cambrian age, as pebbles derived from them are found abundantly in the basal conglomerates of the unconformably overlying Cambrian sediments.

III. THE CAMBRIAN SYSTEM

THE EARLIEST Cambrian deposits were laid down upon an ancient platform of Pre-Cambrian rocks in an extensive sea or ocean that stretched from the (present) Atlantic sea-board of North America eastwards across what is now Wales to Scandinavia and south-east Europe.

Before the Cambrian period in North Wales, this platform was denuded deeply enough to expose in different places the various members of the Bedded Series and their metamorphosed representatives, the plutonic intrusions, and the younger volcanic series of the mainland. As Cambrian times advanced, the area covered by the sea gradually increased, and the first coarse littoral and nearshore deposits became buried under strata that accumulated in deeper and more open waters. Before the end of Lower Cambrian times the basin of deposition (a geosyncline) was well established, its central parts receiving thick piles of terrigenous deposits which are exposed at the present day as greywackes, flags, shales, and slates.

During Cambrian times North Wales was occupied by a principal trough of deposition which lay in the region of the present Harlech Dome, where some 15,000 ft of sediment accumulated. To the south-east the existence of shallows or a nearby shoreline is indicated by the rocks of Shropshire, at least during Lower and Middle Cambrian times. The north-western margin of the trough is not now recognisable, the evidence being destroyed in Anglesey by pre-Ordovician uplift and erosion (Fig. 11, p.28).

The ancient platform of Pre-Cambrian rocks across which the Lower Palaeozoic sea advanced was far from being perfectly level, and inequalities in the height of its surface resulted in some parts being submerged before others; and the drowned landscape is to be imagined as being not greatly dissimilar from an archipelagic or a ria coast of the present day, with scattered islands and slightly submerged reefs. A thick bed of grit or conglomerate may thus have been deposited near a shore contemporaneously with a much thinner bed of fine-grained sandstone or shale farther out to sea. Moreover, the sinking of the geosynclinal floor and the deepening of the transgressive seas were not absolutely regular and uninterrupted: at times deposition outran subsidence, and occasionally there were positive uplifts of the sea floor. The establishment and growth of the geosyncline was an intermittent process, the pulsatory movements by which it grew being reflected in the nature and persistence of the sediments that accumulated on its floor. Intervals of shallowing are indicated by the occurrence of beds of sandstone, grit, and conglomerate and discontinuities of deposition by unconformable junctions or the absence of fossil zones. The rhythmic movements of subsidence are marked by rhythms of sedimentation; indeed, alternations of the different types of sediment constitute the evidence upon which the rhythms of subsidence are inferred, and on their occurrence the system may be subdivided into a large number of lithological groups, which display a rhythmic variation in lithology.

The Cambrian rocks crop out in three main areas. The largest is the complex anticline of the Harlech Dome in Merioneth. It is separated by the Snowdon syncline from the Nantlle–Llanberis–Bethesda outcrop, which runs along the south-eastern flank of the Padarn ridge. The third outcrop forms a small inlier along the cliffs of St. Tudwal's Peninsula in Lleyn.

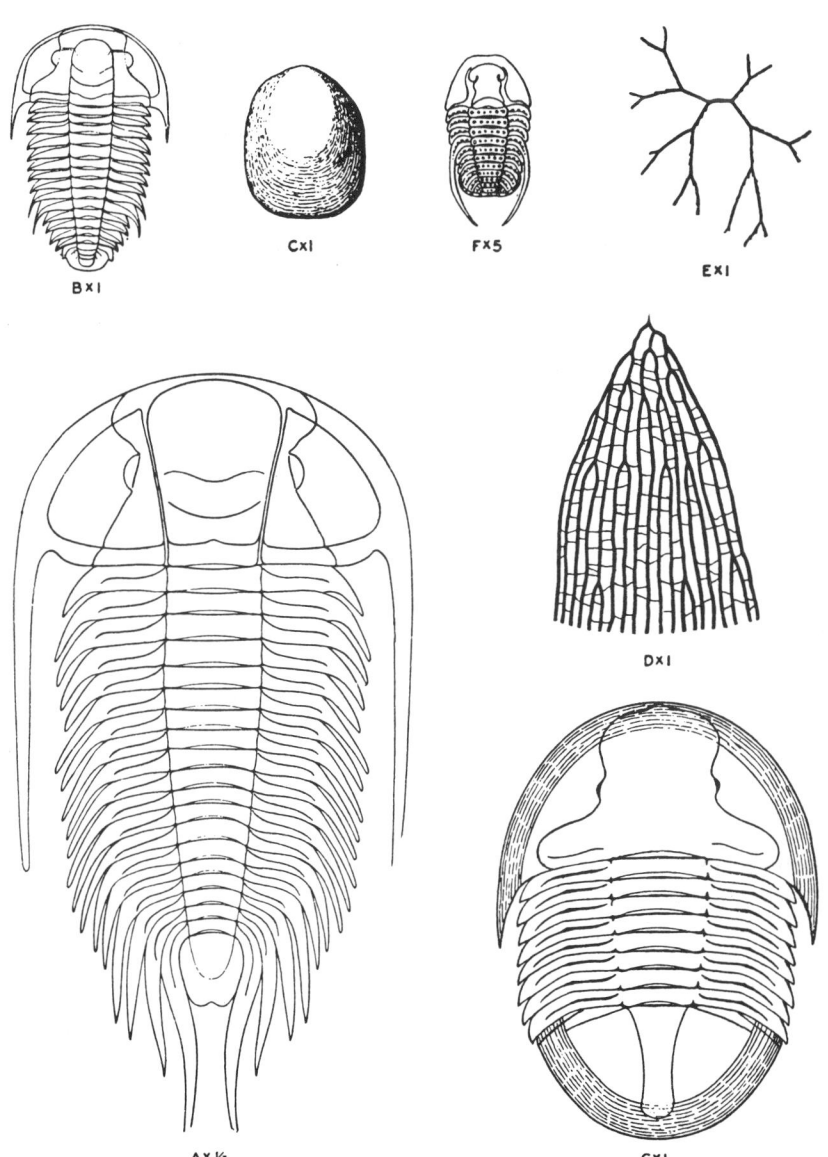

FIG. 5: *Cambrian fossils*

A, *Paradoxides davidis* Salter, Middle Cambrian; B, *Olenus cataractes* Salter, Maentwrog Beds, Upper Cambrian; C, *Lingulella davisii* (M'Coy), Ffestiniog Beds, Upper Cambrian; D, *Dictyonema flabelliforme* (Eichwald), Tremadoc Slates, Upper Cambrian; E, *Clonograptus tenellus* (Linnarsson), Tremadoc Slates; F, *Shumardia pusilla* (Sars), Tremadoc Slates; G, *Asaphellus homfrayi* (Salter), Tremadoc Slates.

THE HARLECH DOME

The Harlech Dome and its borders (Fig. 6), described in detail by Matley and Wilson, display the thickest succession of Cambrian rocks to be seen in Britain; they form a barren and desolate tract, much of it almost without habitation, with high, rugged, block-like mountains where thick bands of grit and conglomerate come to the surface (see Pl. III; and Fig. 7, p. 21). The older members are found in elongate anticlinal cores in the heart of the Dome, the younger ones crop out from Criccieth to Cader Idris in successive peripheral arcs, often broken by faults and distorted by minor folds, but on the whole fairly regular and complete.

The general succession, determined by Sedgwick, Ramsay, Salter, and Belt, is in descending order as follows:

4. Tremadoc Slates.
3. *Lingula* Flags.
2. Menevian or Clogau Shales.
1. Harlech Beds: a dominantly gritty series with shales and slates.

Elsewhere in Britain the subdivisions of the Cambrian system are essentially based on the nature of the contained fossils, mainly trilobites (see Fig. 5); but in the Harlech country fossils are rare or absent in the Harlech Beds and uncommon in the *Lingula* Flags (except the uppermost member), and stratal grouping was mainly established on marked changes in lithology. Thus no trilobites of the Lower Cambrian Olenellid stage or of the Middle Cambrian Solva stage have been found in the Harlech Beds—a group some 6,000–7,000 ft thick, almost completely unfossiliferous—and while *Paradoxides*, together with *Agnostus*, *Ptychoparia*, and *Meneviella*, occurs in the Menevian Clogau Shales, it is not widespread through the series. The *Lingula* Flags at certain horizons contain an Olenid trilobite fauna, including *Olenus* itself; and in them, too, the brachiopod *Lingulella davisii* occurs commonly. The Tremadoc Beds contain *Shumardia* and Olenid trilobites (*Angelina*), together with early members of the typically Ordovician family of Asaphid trilobites (*Asaphellus*, *Niobella*); and are noteworthy as yielding the first graptolites of the British succession (*Dictyonema* and *Clonograptus*).

The Harlech Beds. The Harlech Beds, the details of which have been largely made known through the work of Lapworth, Andrew, Cox, Wells, Wilson, and Matley, clearly display the oscillatory rhythms of sedimentation characteristic of the Lower Palaeozoic geosyncline. In ascending sequence they comprise the Dolwen Grit, the Llanbedr Slates, the Rhinog Grits, the Manganese Shales, the Barmouth Grits, and the Gamlan Shales: together they reach a thickness of nearly 7,000 ft and contain a variety of arenaceous and argillaceous deposits.

The Dolwen Grit, felspathic greywackes, siltstones, and pebbly grits with some shales, is exposed to a thickness of 500 ft; but its base is nowhere seen, the arching of the Harlech Dome not being sufficiently acute and erosion not having proceeded sufficiently deeply to expose the floor. It is not certain, therefore, that the Grit rests on Pre-Cambrian rocks, and it may not be the oldest member of the Cambrian sequence: in detailed lithology it differs appreciably from the Cilgwyn Conglomerate, which visibly forms the Cambrian base at Nantlle, though (like most of the other Cambrian grits) it contains an abundance of derived Pre-Cambrian fragments.

The cleaved blue and purple Llanbedr Slates, which succeed the Dolwen Grit, are about 300 ft thick in the heart of the Dome but increase to 700 ft near

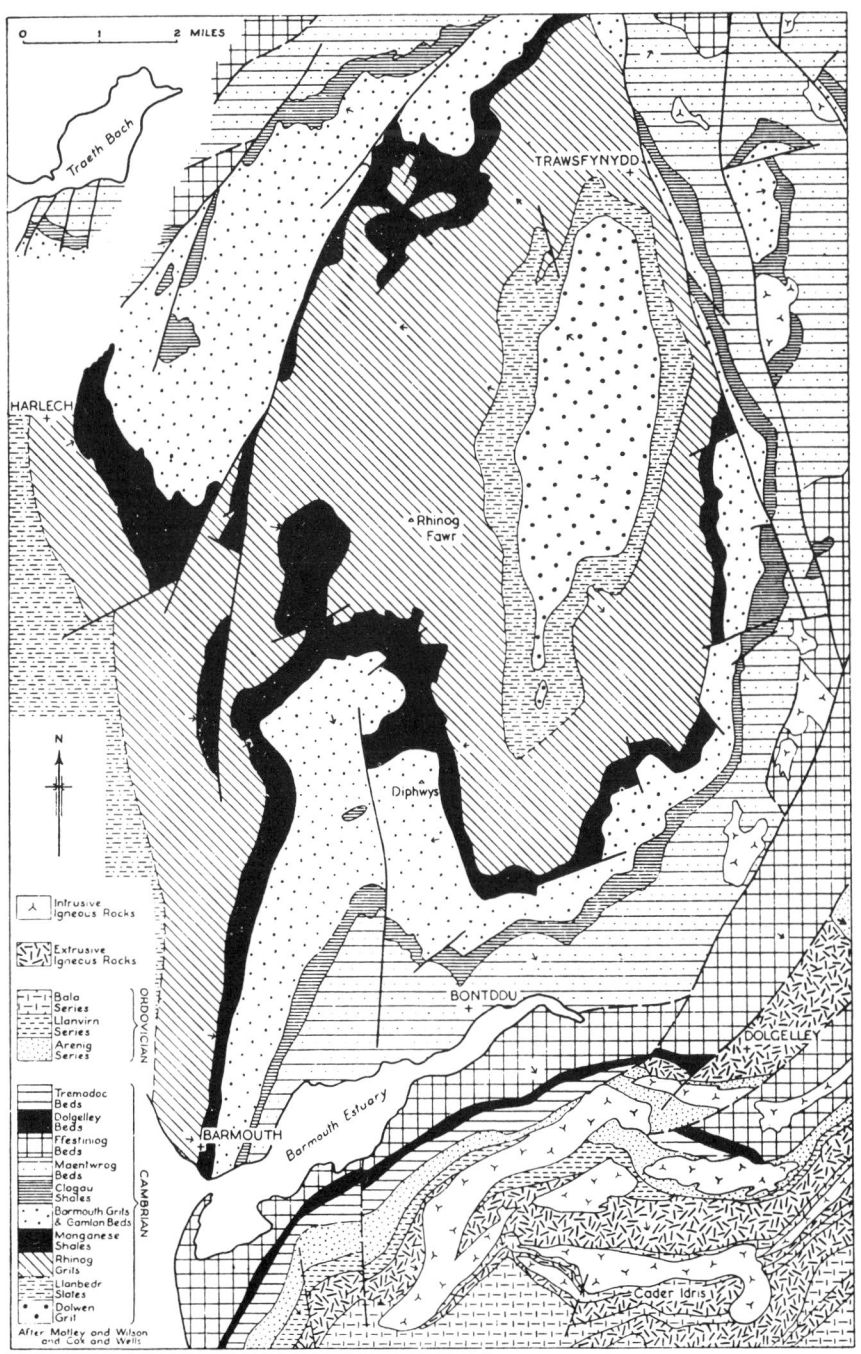

FIG. 6: *Geological map of the Harlech Dome and the Cader Idris range*

Llanbedr. They are marred commercially by the frequent occurrence of ribs of siltstone, sandstone, and grit which cause them to split irregularly along the cleavage planes.

The Rhinog Grits, 1,200 ft thick in the west, 2,500 ft in the centre of the Dome, form the dominant member of the Harlech Beds. Tough and massive grey-wackes, sandstones, and grits with shaly partings, they form some of the higher hills of the Dome, including Rhinog Fawr and Rhinog Fach, Craig Gwion, and Craig-y-ganllwyd. Woodland has described their lithology in detail: following Greenly, he has recorded from conglomeratic layers a variety of derived pebbles, many of which agree closely with rocks of the Mona Complex. Some of the sediments show graded bedding and other signs of deposition by turbidity currents.

The overlying Manganese or Hafotty Shales, 400–800 ft thick, are distinguished from the Grits by their very fine grain. The beds are striped and banded green and grey mudstones with only occasional sandy layers of which the most prominent, occurring near the base, is the Manganese Grit reaching a thickness of 200 ft. The manganese ore that gives its name to the group occurs as a hard flinty band near the base: it is mainly composed, as Woodland has shown, of rhodochrosite, dialogite, and spessartite-garnet, with some small amounts of rhodonite and pyrolusite. Its red or purple colour is due to a small proportion of haematite. The ore appears to be an original deposit (though there has been some later chemical reconstruction) perhaps as a colloidal mixture of manganese carbonate with clay and silica. It suggests deposition in the very quiet waters of an enclosed basin or 'lagoon' protected from the influx of much terrigenous detritus, the manganese enrichment being by precipitation from concentrated solutions. In contrast with the more normal sediments it may indicate strong shallowing and a non-marine environment. The ore has been worked in numerous small levels, but, the content of impurity being comparatively high and transport difficulties being great, economic exploitation is not practicable at the present time.

The succeeding Barmouth Grits, 400–600 ft thick, are very similar in lithology to the Rhinog Grits, and similarly form the main mass of a number of the higher hills—Y Garn, Diphwys, and Llawllech. They are coarse conglomeratic grits with large pebbles of white and rose quartz and common rounded fragments of fresh felspar: these mixed constituents suggest that they also derived their material mainly from some mass of gneissose and granitic rocks. Kopstein has suggested that signs of transport direction indicate a source of origin for the coarser fragments in Pre-Cambrian masses to the south or south-west; but such a mode of deposition is at variance with what is known of the palaeogeography of the geosyncline.

The Gamlan Shales, about 800 ft thick, are finer-grained representatives of the same rock-suite as the Barmouth Grits: amongst the true shales are interbedded numerous bands of grit and flagstone, of which the Cefn-coch Grit at the top is prominent. Some of the mudstones contain abundant worm tubes (so-called ' fucoids ').

The divisions of the Harlech Beds are more readily distinguished in the western outcrops of the Dome. Traced eastwards they tend to lose their indi-vidual characteristics, mainly by a relative increase in the coarser constituents. This suggests that contemporary land lay at no great distance towards the east or north-east, though O. T. Jones has pointed out that the evidence is not uniformly consistent and the derived pebbles of Anglesey type may indicate contemporary erosion of a tract lying to the north or north-west.

(A.6514)

A. The Harlech Dome

Plate III

B. Landscape in the Harlech Dome

(A.6506)

The Menevian Beds. The Gamlan Shales pass upwards into the Menevian or Clogau Shales, a series, 300 ft thick, of very fine-grained, black, pyritous, cleaved mudstones that are easily traceable, because of their low-lying and relatively fertile outcrop, around the flanks of the Dome. They are particularly noteworthy as the earliest deposits of the Harlech Dome to yield a rich fossil fauna: the fossils include the trilobites *Paradoxides hicksii* and *davidis*, *Meneviella venulosa*, *Eodiscus punctatus*, *Ptychoparia homfrayi*, and Agnostids, and the horny brachiopods *Acrothele maculata* and *Lingulella ferruginea*: they indicate an upper Middle Cambrian age.

The Lingula Flags. The argillaceous Clogau Shales are followed by beds relatively quartz-rich though the quartz is of fine grain in flaggy layers. These beds have usually been classified together as the *Lingula* Flags, but they reveal marked variations of sedimentary environment, and on a lithological basis they have been divided into the following groups:

(c) Dolgelley Beds: about 500 ft thick.

(b) Ffestiniog Beds: about 1,500 ft thick.

(a) Maentwrog Beds: about 2,200 ft thick.

The Maentwrog Beds are mainly shales and mudstones, but the lower part (the Vigra Flags about 1,000 ft thick) includes many beds of tough fine-grained light grey micaceous sandstone ('ringers') that contrast in colour with the dark bluish grey shales. The individual beds are not more than a few inches thick and produce in any extended section of the group an appearance of ribbon banding. The ringers are often ripple-marked and current-bedded, and show signs of shallow-water deposition. Fossils found in the upper part of the Vigra Beds include *Olenus gibbosus*, Agnostid trilobites, and *Obolella*-like brachiopods, and worm-casts are abundant. The rocks are therefore of Upper Cambrian age.

The upper strata of the Maentwrog Beds, the Penrhos Slates, show a dying-out of the ringers, and through a thickness of about 1,200 ft the rocks are uniformly blue and black pyritous shales, more or less cleaved, and silty mudstones. Fossils include *Olenus cataractes* and Agnostids.

The Ffestiniog Beds resemble the Vigra Beds in general lithology, notably in the abundance of siliceous ringers, and they suggest even more strongly the rhythms of sedimentation that are the result of the repeated influx of fast-flowing silt-laden turbidity currents. The upper part has yielded the Olenid *Beltella bucephala*, and crowding some of the bedding planes are specimens of *Lingulella davisii*, the horny brachiopod that prompted Sedgwick to give the name *Lingula* Flags to the whole group of rocks.

The Dolgelley Beds, the uppermost member of the *Lingula* Flags, consist of an uninterrupted succession of shales and slates, grey and bluish grey in the lower part, becoming darker and increasingly carbonaceous and pyritous to form the 'Black Band' in the upper. Lithologically they give the impression of having accumulated under euxinic or poorly aerated conditions, but they contain in many bands a relatively rich fauna of benthic organisms including trilobites (notably *Parabolina spinulosa* and *Peltura scarabaeoides*) and brachiopods (*Orusia* [*Orthis*] *lenticularis*).

Near Dolgelley a few beds of volcanic ash and lava appear in the *Lingula* Flags, and may prelude the outburst of igneous activity of Ordovician times.

The Tremadoc Beds. The Tremadoc Beds, occupying the uppermost position in the Cambrian sequence, are somewhat coarser in texture and lighter in colour than the Dolgelley Beds. They consist of a thick monotonous succession of grey and blue mudstones and shales, many of which have been altered to slates.

The slates, however, are poorly cleaved, and have not been so extensively worked as those of the Middle and Lower Cambrian (p. 55). Within the sequence, despite the general lithological similarity throughout, Fearnsides has recognised a number of subdivisions that are distinguished on slight differences in fossils and lithology. These subdivisions (the most characteristic of which is perhaps the *Dictyonema* Band near the base) are traceable with remarkable constancy around the Harlech Dome. Fossils, often much distorted by the cleavage, are relatively common, and include both persistent Cambrian types (Olenid trilobites including *Angelina sedgwickii*) and forerunners of Ordovician families (*Asaphellus homfrayi, Niobella homfrayi*).

In many places some or all of the Tremadoc Beds are absent owing to unconformable overstep by the succeeding Ordovician rocks.

THE LLEYN PENINSULA

A small inlier of Cambrian rocks is seen in St. Tudwal's Peninsula, separated from the main mass of the Harlech Dome by intervening Ordovician rocks and by the sea of the northern part of Cardigan Bay. The succession, described by T. C. Nicholas, is not complete, partly because some of the beds are faulted out, but chiefly because of overstep by the basal Ordovician grits, which rest with marked unconformity upon the underlying strata and in places transgress the outcrops of the Upper and Middle Cambrian and rest upon the Lower (see Fig. 10, p. 26). The preserved sequence is an attenuated representative of that occurring on the western flanks of the Harlech Dome (Fig. 7). All the Tremadoc Beds and some of the *Lingula* Flags are missing, the remaining strata being:

3. *Lingula* Flags. Ffestiniog and Maentwrog Beds, as in the Harlech Dome. The Maentwrog Beds contain *Olenus*.
2. Menevian Beds. The Nant-pig Mudstones. These are the equivalent of the Clogau Shales of the Dome, and consist of the normal succession of blue-black and black pyritous shales and mudstones, with an abundant trilobite fauna including *Paradoxides hicksii*, followed by mudstones representing the lower part of the *P. davidis* Zone. These in turn are followed by a thin grit containing limestone pebbles yielding trilobites indicating the *P. forchhammeri* Zone.
1. Harlech Beds. Divisible into:
    (iv) Caered Mudstones and Flags. Mudstones with green sandstones and flags, the equivalent of the Gamlan Shales. They contain *Paradoxides hicksii* and prove to be of Middle Cambrian age.
    (iii) Cilan Grits. Massive grits with some interbedded mudstones, the equivalent of the Barmouth Grits. They differ from the other members of the St. Tudwal's succession in being thicker than their correlatives in the Harlech country.
    (ii) Mulfran Beds. Blue striped and banded mudstones with manganese ore, the local representatives of the Manganese Shales.
    (i) Hell's Mouth Grits. Massive grits with some interbedded mudstones, the equivalent of the Rhinog Grits. The recent important discovery by Bassett and Walton of a Protolenid trilobite fauna in the upper beds of the group proves the age to be late Lower Cambrian. Presumably therefore the Barmouth–Cilan Grits, and perhaps the Manganese Shales, are wholly or in part of lower Middle Cambrian (Solva) age.

The beds dip towards the east and are therefore separated by an intermediate syncline from the anticline of the Harlech country. To the west any equivalents of the Llanbedr Slates and Dolwen Grit and of any underlying Cambrian

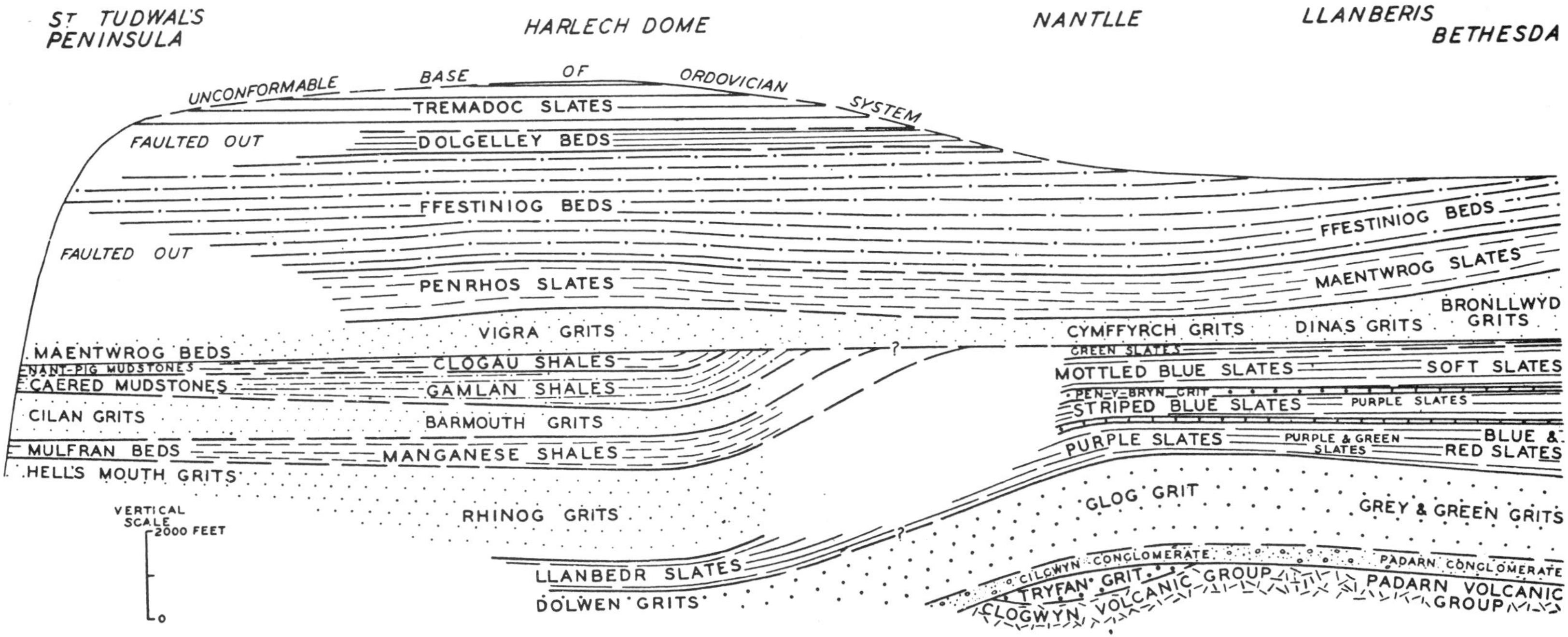

FIG. 7: *Diagram illustrating an interpretation of lateral variations in the Cambrian rocks of North Wales*

The Green Slates of Nantlle and Llanberis are about of the same age (upper Lower Cambrian) as the upper beds of the Hell's Mouth Grits (Rhinog Grits) of St. Tudwal's peninsula; but how the Llanberis Slates as a whole correlate with the Harlech Grit series is unknown. The absence of recognisable Menevian Beds in the outcrops between Nantlle and Bethesda is probably due to overstep by the Cymffyrch and Bronllwyd Grits, which in the diagram are then correlated with the Upper Cambrian Vigra Beds (Lingula Flags); but it is possible that the Bronllwyd Grit (which has yielded no fossils) is the equivalent to the Rhinog Grits, the unconformity then lying at the base of the Maentwrog Slates.

rocks that may be present are hidden beneath the sea of Porth Neigwl, the base of the Hell's Mouth Grits not being seen.

CAERNARVONSHIRE

In the part of North Wales separated from the Harlech Dome by the Snowdon syncline of Ordovician rocks, the Cambrian sediments come to outcrop along the southern flanks of the Bethesda–Penygroes anticlinal ridge of the Pre-Cambrian Padarn and Clogwyn volcanic rocks. A few small patches of what may be Cambrian conglomerates are seen farther north on the north-western flanks of the Bangor ridge, and grits and conglomerates (the Careg-onen Beds) also doubtfully Cambrian in age occur in south-east Anglesey; but mostly in the ground beyond the Padarn ridge Cambrian rocks are absent as a result of strong overstep by Ordovician. On the southern flank of the ridge the slate-belt from Penrhyn through Llanberis to Nantlle is well exposed in a number of large quarries providing excellent sections through nearly the whole of the series, parts of which have been described in detail by Morris and Fearnsides (see Fig. 8).

The earliest deposits, of which no representatives are known in the Harlech Dome, are coarse basal conglomerates, the Cilgwyn and Llyn Padarn conglomerates reaching 500 ft in thickness. They rest directly and with great unconformity on the Pre-Cambrian rocks, and contain abundant pebbles of rhyolite derived from the Clogwyn and Padarn Volcanic Series. They pass upwards gradually into a series of fine grits and quartzites, the Glog and St. Anne's Grits, that attain a thickness of 2,000 ft. As deeper-water conditions were established, shales and mudstones became the chief types of deposit: as now seen they are usually metamorphosed to slates. The slates reach a thickness of about 2,300 ft near Llanberis, 2,800 ft near Bethesda, the continuous succession of argillaceous rocks being broken only by comparatively thin ribs of sandstone, of which the Dorothea Grit of Nantlle (100 ft thick) (equivalent to the Red Grit or Gwenithfaen-goch of Penrhyn) and the Penybryn Grit (200 ft thick) are the chief.

The slates and the underlying grits are completely unfossiliferous except in their uppermost beds, where the Green Slate group of Llanberis has yielded a trilobite fauna, including *Pseudatops* [*Conocoryphe*] *viola*, that is regarded by Howell and Stubblefield as of late Lower Cambrian (Protolenid) age. It is thus difficult precisely to equate the slates with any of the exposed rocks of the Harlech Dome (see Fig. 7). They are of approximately the same age as the upper part of the Rhinog (Hell's Mouth) Grits, from which however they are very different in lithology; and it is not easy to correlate the Llanbedr Slates of Harlech with the lower part of the Llanberis Slates, or the Dolwen Grit with the Glog Grit, unless there is lateral passage of the Rhinog Grits into the main mass of the Llanberis Slates. This would imply a source for the coarser material towards the south or south-east, whereas the internal evidence of current transport provided by the Hell's Mouth Grits strongly indicates a source to the north or north-east in a land-mass composed of Mona-type rocks.

There is corresponding difficulty in dating the beds above the slates. These beds consist of coarse sandstones, grits, and conglomerates (the Bronllwyd Grit of Penryhn, the Dinas Grit of Llanberis, the Cymffyrch Grit of Nantlle) some 600 to 1,600 ft in thickness, and are very similar lithologically to the Rhinog Grits on the one hand, with which they have been correlated by O. T. Jones, and the Vigra Grits on the other, with which they have been correlated by

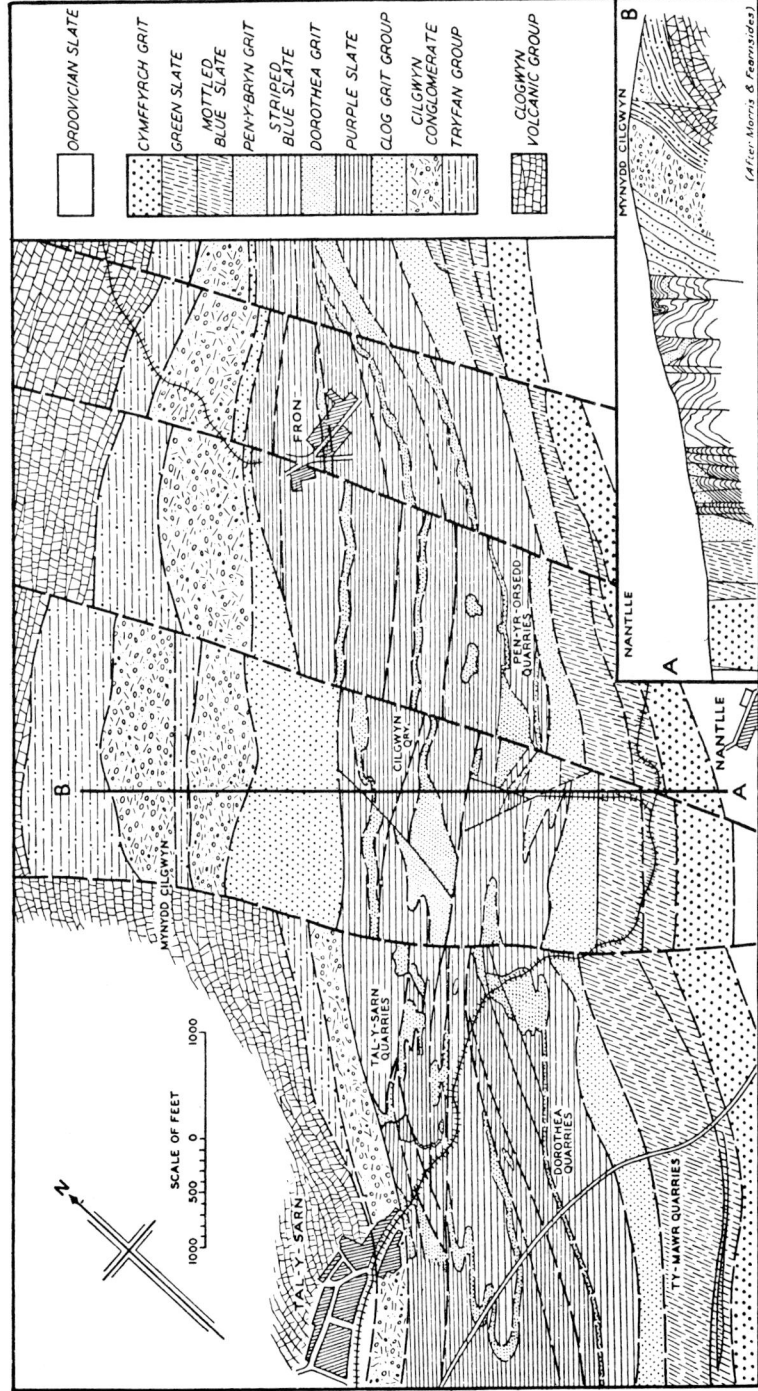

FIG. 8: *Map and section of the Cambrian rocks in the neighbourhood of Nantlle*

The diagram is simplified, and does not indicate the numerous minor igneous intrusions of Ordovician age which cut the rocks.

Morris and Fearnsides. Near Bethesda the grits are conglomeratic at their base and rest with non-sequence upon the slate group: the local absence of any beds recognisable as equivalent to the Middle Cambrian rocks of the Harlech Dome and St. Tudwal's Peninsula is thus explained if the Bronllwyd Grit is regarded as the lateral equivalent of the Vigra Grits, resting with unconformable overstep on the Lower Cambrian Slates. In accordance with this view, the Bronllwyd Grit is followed in expected sequence by slates of Maentwrog type, overlain by fossiliferous Ffestiniog Beds. If on the other hand the Bronllwyd Grit should prove to be the local representative of the Rhinog Grits, the Middle Cambrian rocks are presumably overstepped by the basal members of the Maentwrog-type slates, and the Vigra Grits are missing by overlap. A derived inference is that a land mass lay along and to the north of the Padarn ridge in late Middle Cambrian times, to define the local strandline of the contemporary geosyncline.

Compacted between the massive Pre-Cambrian igneous rocks and Lower Cambrian grits of the Padarn ridge on the one hand and the Ordovician grits and igneous rocks of the Snowdon syncline on the other, the shales of the Cambrian outcrop between Nantlle, Llanberis, and Penrhyn were altered to slates during the Caledonian orogeny, in the manner described on p. 55. These slates, unlike the Llanbedr Shales, are of excellent quality commercially, being almost free from interbedded sandy layers; and they have been quarried and mined on an enormous scale (Pl. IV). The various bands of slate differ slightly in lithological character, in colour and chemical composition, and in the perfection of cleavage, and have consequently been given special names (corresponding approximately to different geological horizons). The sequence of slates at Bethesda, and the structural relations (showing the independence of cleavage and folding), are represented in Fig. 9.

MINERALS IN THE CAMBRIAN ROCKS

Apart from the ore of the Manganese Shales and some of the pisolitic iron-ore (p. 40), which are bedded sediments probably of contemporaneous or pene-contemporaneous origin, the Cambrian rocks of North Wales are notable for the occurrence of secondary metalliferous lodes. These usually occur as quartz veins more or less vertical and having a general north-east to south-west (caledonoid) or north to south trend. They are impregnated with sulphides of copper, iron, zinc, arsenic, antimony, and lead, together with free gold.

The veins cut all the strata from the Barmouth Grits to the Ffestiniog Beds inclusive, but the chief occurrences that have been worked are confined almost entirely to the Menevian Clogau Shales. They are closely associated with the small igneous intrusions that are numerous in the district, and are probably the products of crystallization of the last fluids of the cooling igneous magmas. Like the intrusions, therefore, the veins are almost certainly of Ordovician age, although nowadays exposed in the midst of Cambrian sediments. The minerals were doubtless precipitated when the ascending solutions came into contact with strata containing pyrites, of which considerable quantities exist in the fine-grained Clogau Shales.

The different lodes vary greatly in richness, and within any one lode the distribution of the minerals, dependent on very local causes, is highly irregular. It is therefore difficult to forecast with any certainty the yield likely to be produced from any particular vein, mining operations are consequently inclined to be speculative, and the ore-field is moribund.

Plate IV

(MN2766)

A. Penrhyn slate quarry

B. Dinorwic slate quarry

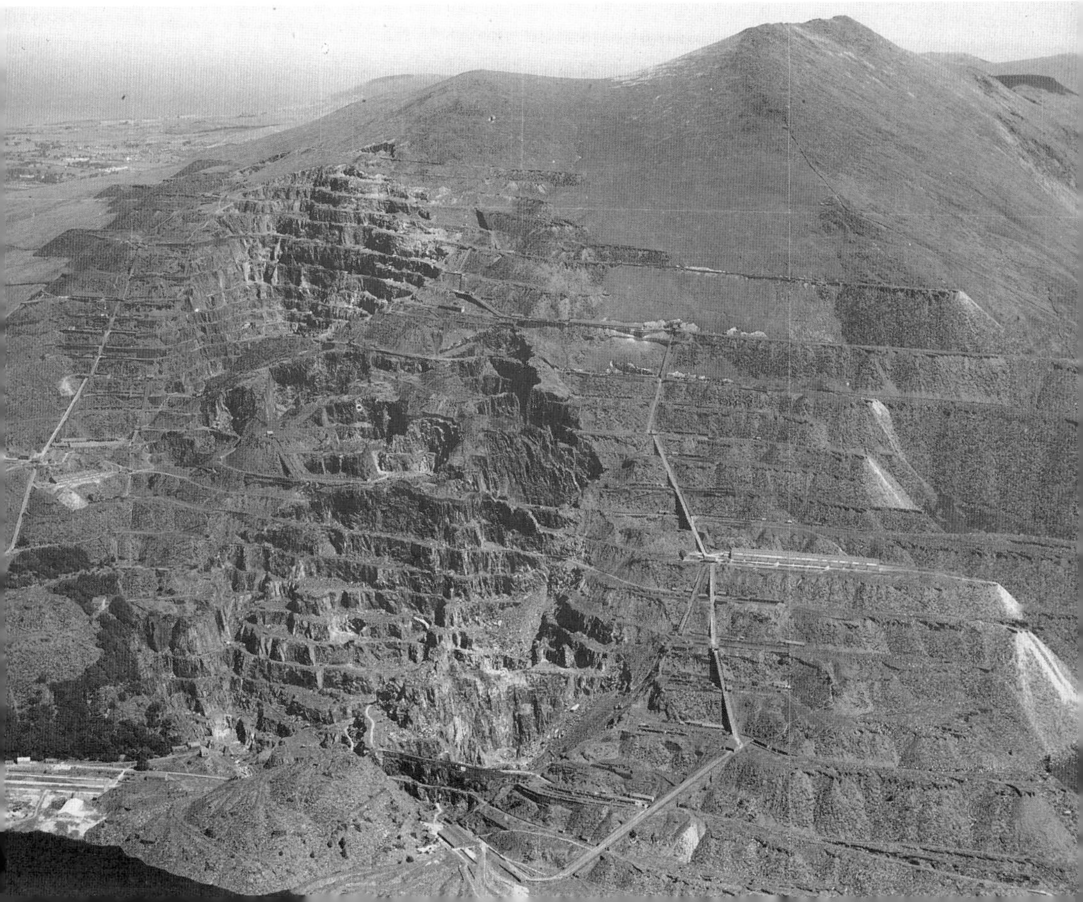

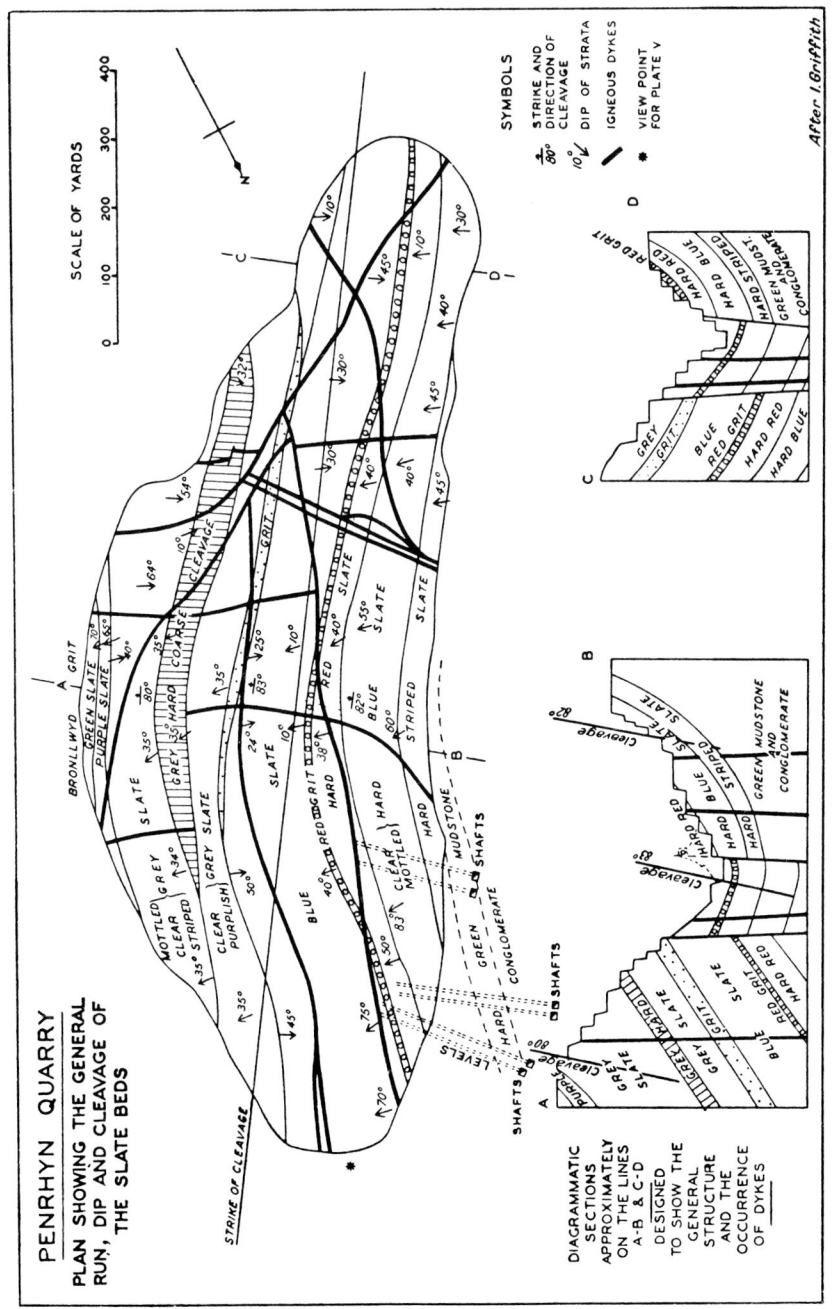

Fig. 9: *Plan and sections of the Penrhyn slate quarry, Bethesda*

IV. THE ORDOVICIAN SYSTEM

BASAL UNCONFORMITY

THE LOWER PALAEOZOIC geosyncline suffered a marked shrinkage at the close of the Cambrian period, so that continuity of deposition into Ordovician times was restricted to small areas. At present transitional deposits occur mainly about the village of Tremadoc but even there, where some of the highest Cambrian rocks known in Britain are found, a sharp lithological change occurs at the Tremadoc–Arenig junction and the appearance of conformity may be illusory. Elsewhere in North Wales more or less great thicknesses of the underlying rocks were removed by erosion before the re-advance of the Ordovician sea: the recognition of this Ordovician overstep, of which he first became aware in the Llanberis district, was one of Ramsay's most valuable contributions to an understanding of the local Lower Palaeozoic geology.

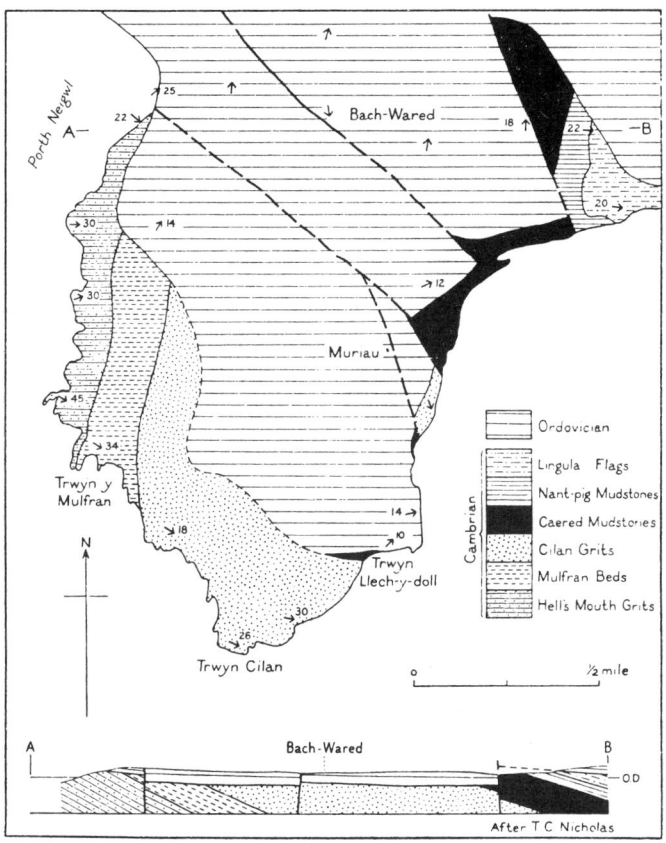

FIG. 10: *Geological map and section of the southern part of St. Tudwal's Peninsula*

26

On the flanks of the Harlech Dome the Tremadoc Beds are usually present, but local thicknesses vary, and while the sub-Ordovician unconformity is nowhere apparent in a discrepancy in dip, a general impression is given of planed undulations in the Cambrian rocks on which the basal Ordovician rest. Near the Dyfi Estuary, however, B. Jones has shown that the transgression cuts out nearly 1,000 ft of Tremadoc Beds in a mile or two, while north-east of Dolgelley the Tremadoc Series and the underlying Dolgelley Beds are missing in places, the basal Arenig rocks resting on Ffestiniog Beds.

The magnitude of the unconformity is, however, best seen in the north-western outcrops. Nicholas has demonstrated in St. Tudwal's Peninsula that the Ordovician rocks in a distance of little over a mile rest transgressively on various members of the Cambrian from *Lingula* Flags in the east to Hell's Mouth Grits (Rhinog Grits) in the west (Fig. 10). A few miles farther west in Lleyn the Cambrian beds are completely overstepped and the Ordovician rests on various members of the Pre-Cambrian complex (see Fig. 11). Similar relations are displayed in the north-western flanks of the Snowdon syncline, where the absence of Tremadoc and Dolgelley Beds is attributable to the same Ordovician overstep. Between the Padarn Ridge and the Menai Straits Cambrian rocks are unknown except perhaps in the Bangor–Caernarvon tract where small inliers of what may be basal Cambrian conglomerates emerge in places from beneath the Arenig grits, which otherwise rest on various members of the Arvonian Pre-Cambrian mass. No Cambrian rocks are certainly known to occur in Anglesey (though the Careg-onen Beds of Red Wharf Bay appear to occur in residual pockets beneath overstepping Arenig rocks), their absence being emphasized by the thick basal Ordovician conglomerates containing abundant pebbles of quartzite, gneiss, schist, and granite derived from the very local source of the Mona Complex (Pl. VA).

This major unconformity, implying the local removal of many thousands of feet of Cambrian rocks and so reflecting a change in contemporary geography brought about by widespread elevation and then subsidence at the close of Cambrian times, is accompanied by the sudden replacement of the relatively deep-water pelagic shales and mudstones of the Tremadoc Beds by the coarse flags, sandstones, grits and conglomerates of the basal Ordovician Garth Grit. As Ordovician times progressed, however, the geosyncline again widened and deepened, the sediments, particularly the graptolitic shales of later Ordovician age, indicating deposition under pelagic conditions. For much of Ordovician times the sediments least affected by the influx of coarse gritty and sandy detritus, and by volcanic action, were deposited in the neighbourhood of the present Anglesey; and, as in Cambrian times, one of the main shorelines lay not far to the south and east of North Wales.

ROCK TYPES

The Ordovician sediments are characterized by an abundance of trilobites; they also contain many brachiopods and a prolific fauna of graptolites (Fig. 12). The latter group made its first appearance (with *Dictyonema*) in the Tremadoc Beds, and by Ordovican times had become so abundant, and displayed such great variety, that its members are even more useful than the trilobites for subdividing the succession into stages and zones, and so for correlating rocks of different areas. The various groups of animals are not found scattered indiscriminately through the Ordovician rocks, but, like modern organisms, some preferred one

GW B

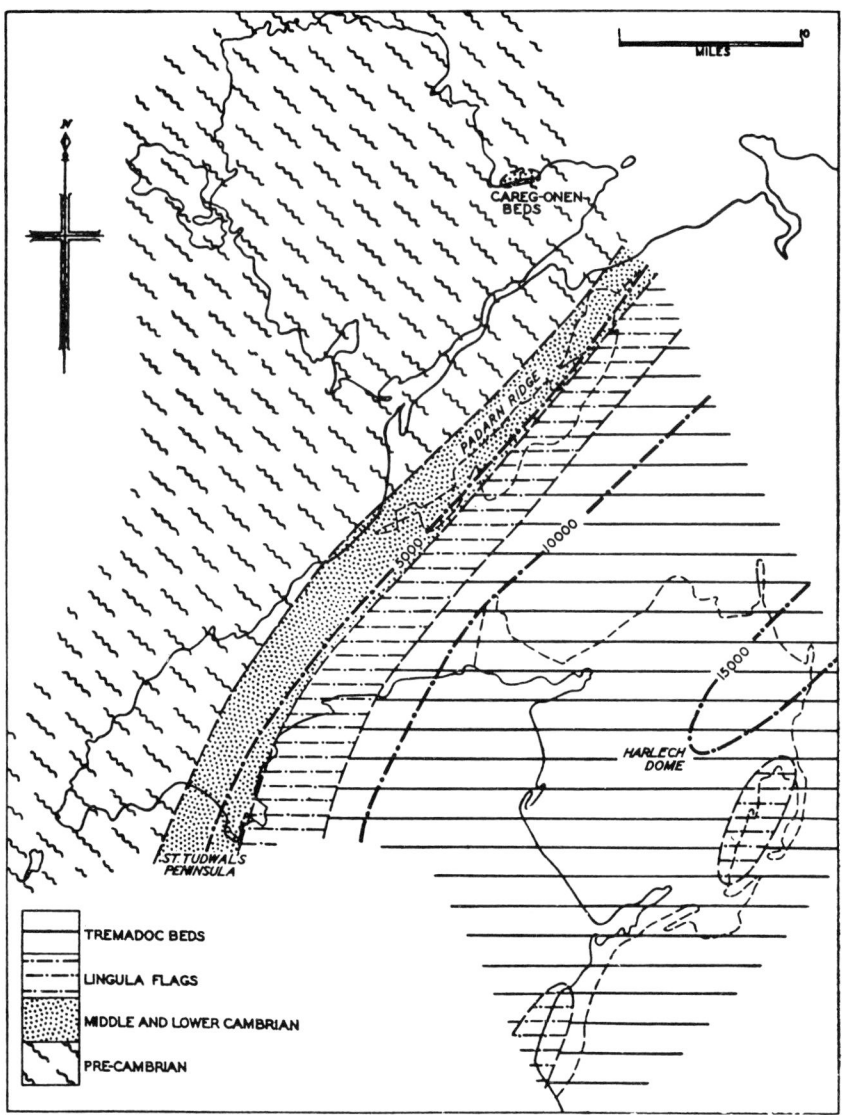

FIG. 11: *Outline map illustrating Ordovician overstep in North Wales*
The map shows residual thickness-contours (isopachs) at 5000-ft intervals in the Cambrian rocks,
and the geology of the eroded Cambrian rocks upon which the basal Ordovician grits
were deposited in North Wales. Some of the lines are conjectural. The absence of Cambrian
sediments in western Lleyn and in the ground north of the Padarn ridge is a measure of
the magnitude of the pre-Ordovician movements and of the intensity of pre-Ordovician
erosion. The present-day Cambrian outcrop is indicated. In part after O. T. Jones and
R. M. Shackleton.

habitat, some another. Thus the trilobites and brachiopods (the shelly fauna)
are found chiefly in the sandy or muddy shallow-water (neritic) deposits, while
the planktonic or pseudoplanktonic graptolites are characteristic of the black
shales and muds of the pelagic parts of the trough or of lagoonal euxinic environments. The rhythms of change in conditions of deposition that occurred
throughout Ordovician times are therefore reflected not only in lithological

(A.1221)

A. Unconformity in Anglesey

B. Scarps in the Berwyn Hills

Plate V

(A.3676)

alternations of the strata, but also in parallel alternations of the contained fossils: strong currents, or well aerated and refreshed sea water, or a shelving open coast encouraged and favoured the immigration and abundant growth of shelly forms; water becoming deep, or poorly ventilated, or relatively stagnant and poisoned, led to the formation of dark-coloured sediments rich in fossilised graptolites. A third broad kind of sediment falls into the greywacke suite of rocks: it consists of ill-sorted detritus forming a dark impure sandstone, and appears to have been formed by deposition from fast-flowing turbidity currents that poured their rock fragments onto the sea-floor often in a belt lying between the shelly neritic muds and sands and the graptolitic shales. Because of the manner of their formation they are usually without indigenous fossils. Obvious difficulties ensue in correlating rocks of these contrasted facies.

Supplementing the effects of the repeated earth-movements (and perhaps related to them), and contributing to the variations in the sediments, were the volcanic outbursts of the Ordovician period. The volcanoes, partly submarine, were mainly localized as vent-outbursts in independent centres in different parts of the area, and they were active during different, but sometimes overlapping, intervals of time. There were separate centres about Cader Idris, the Arans, the Arenigs, Manod and the Moelwyns, Capel Curig, Conway, and Snowdon, in the Lleyn Peninsula, and in the neighbourhood of the Berwyns. In the Cader Idris range (see Fig. 13) and the Moelwyn Hills vulcanicity was intermittent from Lower until the beginning of Upper Ordovician times; in the Arenig–Conway–Snowdon–Lleyn country and the Berwyns the chief outbursts were in Upper Ordovician times. There is much lateral variation in thickness of the volcanic rocks, the greatest piles naturally being found in the immediate neighbourhoods of the volcanic vents. Moreover, while lavas and coarse agglomerates are characteristic of the areas in the vicinity of the main centres, finer tuffs, covering more extensive areas, are the chief types found deposited farther away. Some of the ashes appear to have been transported in *nuées ardentes*, great clouds of hot gases that carried lava droplets and all but the largest fragments and ' bombs ' in violently turbulent streams down the volcanic slopes and spread them out on the lower ground in enormous 'delta' fans: on settling many of the smaller droplets fused with their neighbours to form welded tuffs (ignimbrites). There can be little doubt that the peaks of the larger volcanoes emerged above sea level to form groups of small islands dotted over North Wales, each with its fringing beach and each subject to rapid erosion by wave attack. Below sea level the volcanic products became incorporated in the rock sequence when volcanic action died down and were buried under normal sediments. In the nature of the case the lavas traced from their volcanic sources end abruptly at the limits of flow, but the tuffs merge laterally into and mix with normal marine sediments or with tuffs from other volcanic centres. The volcanic rock types vary from rhyolitic to basaltic.

Associated with the extrusive volcanic rocks are abundant large and small intrusions (stocks, dykes, and sills) that cut through them and. the sediments, and now weather out as rugged crags or escarpments. They consist of rock-types closely similar to those of the lavas and tuffs and vary between acid granites, porphyries, and felsites, and basic and sub-basic diorites, gabbros, and dolerites.

The Ordovician rocks now form extensive tracts surrounding the Harlech Dome, sweeping in a half-circle from Cader Idris and the Talyllyn valley through the Arans into the Bala country, the Arenigs, and the Moelwyns. They occupy the complex syncline of Snowdonia, which extends north-eastwards

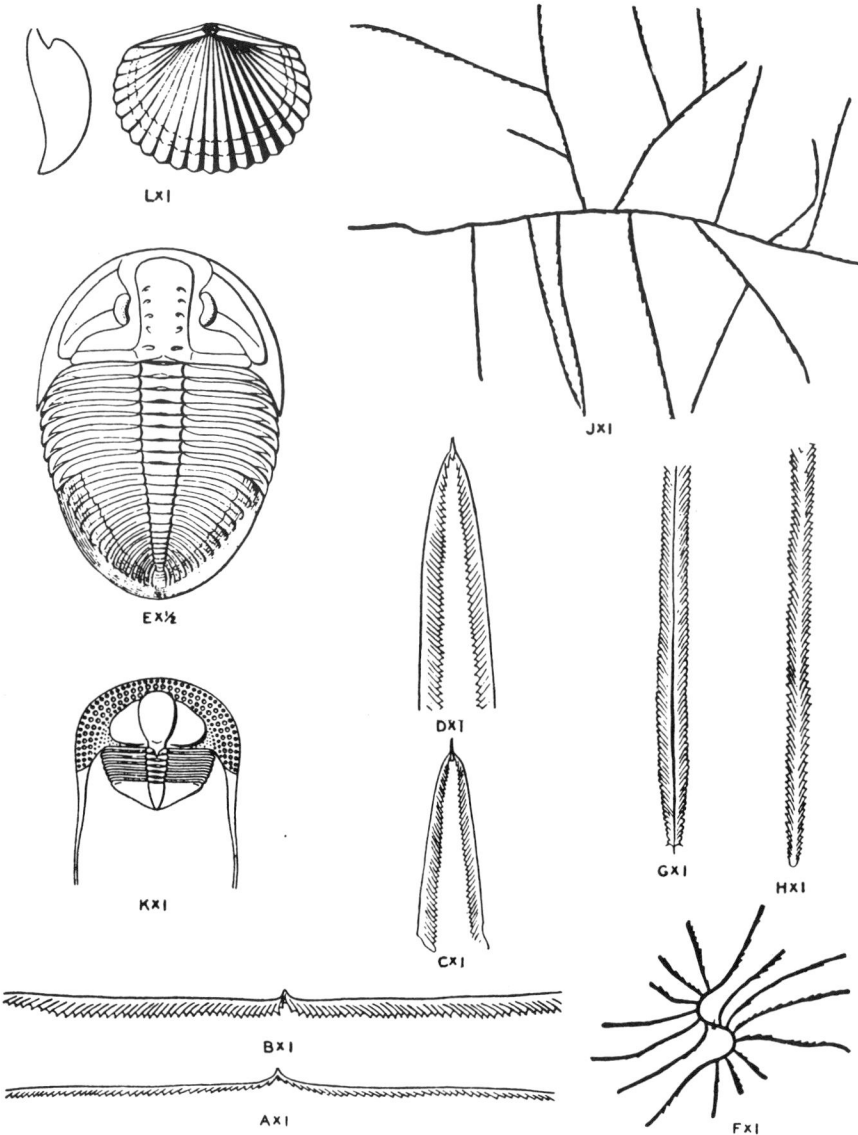

FIG. 12: *Ordovician fossils*
(Graptolite drawings after Elles and Wood).

Arenig Series, **A**, *Didymograptus extensus* (Hall); **B**, *D. hirundo* Salter. Llanvirn Series, **C**, *D. bifidus* (Hall); **D**, *D. murchisoni* (Beck). Llandeilo Series, **E**, *Ogygiocarella [Ogygia] debuchii* (Brongniart). Caradoc Series, **F**, *Nemagraptus gracilis* (Hall); **G**, *Diplograptus [Mesograptus] multidens* Elles and Wood; **H**, *Orthograptus truncatus* Lapworth; **J**, *Pleurograptus linearis* Carruthers*; **K**, *Cryptolithus [Trinucleus] sp.*; **L**, *Orthis (Dinorthis) flabellulum* J. de C. Sowerby.

*This species has not been recorded from North Wales but the zone is said to occur.

into the heights about Conway and Penmaenmawr, and westwards as the greater part of the Lleyn Peninsula (see Pl. XII). Separated by a narrow tongue of Silurian rocks (the northward continuation of the Central Wales syncline), the Berwyn Hills rise to the east as another anticlinal dome, secondary to that of Harlech, but without Cambrian rocks exposed in its core. In Anglesey, extensive Ordovician outliers rest on the Pre-Cambrian rocks of the Mona Complex.

The system is divided by means of the graptolites and trilobites into four principal series:

4. BALA. Characterized by a mixed fauna of Leptograptid, Dicranograptid, and Diplograptid graptolites, of which typical members are *Nemagraptus gracilis*, *Climacographtus peltifer*, *Dicranograptus clingani*, and *Dicellograptus anceps*. The Lower Bala is distinguished as the Caradoc Series, the Upper Bala as the Ashgill.

3. LLANDEILO. Characterized by a mixed fauna of Leptograptid, Dicranograptid, and Diplograptid graptolites, of which *Glyptograptus teretiusculus* is the typical member.

2. LLANVIRN. Characterized by a Dichograptid fauna, of which the principal members are the tuning-fork graptolites *Didymograptus bifidus* and *Didymograptus murchisoni*.

1. ARENIG. Characterized by a Dichograptid fauna, of which the principal members are *Tetragraptus* and the extensiform graptolites *Didymograptus extensus* and *Didymograptus hirundo*.

ARENIG SERIES

The earliest Arenig rocks of North Wales are the volcanic lavas and tuffs of the Rhobell Fawr centre, described by A. K. Wells. They rest with discordance upon various horizons down to the Ffestiniog Beds of the Upper Cambrian, and were themselves deeply eroded (as subaerial accumulations) before the deposition of the earliest local Ordovician marine sediments (the Garth Grit) upon them. The outburst was largely explosive, and the products are coarse tuffs and agglomerates, with relatively minor lava flows. The rock-types are the sub-basic andesites.

The succeeding Arenig sediments suggest a progressive deepening of the waters of deposition, for, commencing with the coarse-grained sandy and conglomeratic Garth Grit, they show a broad upward passage through flag-stones into fine graptolitic shales in the higher beds. On the southern and eastern flanks of the Harlech Dome the basal arenaceous beds are only some 200 to 300 ft thick, but to the north and north-west with stronger Ordovician overstep they are much thicker. They attain their maximum development in Anglesey, where the basal conglomerates, resting on a deeply eroded surface of rocks of the Mona Complex, reach a thickness of 3,000 ft in places (see Fig. 22, p. 54). They are overlain by 1,200 ft of finer sediments (the *Tetragraptus* Shales). In Lleyn the series consists of the *Didymograptus extensus* Flags (sometimes with an equivalent of the Garth Grit at the base) some 400 ft thick, followed by a group of striped shales with *Tetragraptus* several hundred feet thick. South-west of the Cader Idris range there is a broadly similar succession, which B. Jones has described as thickening to some 1,500 ft on the coast near Tonfanau, mainly by an increased development of sandy beds. Many of the sediments are well-sorted, and in the presence of current bedding and a rapid variation in grain size they give indication of deposition in shallow water.

A characteristic fossil of the basal Arenig sediments in most of the outcrops is the polyzoan *Bolopora undosa*.

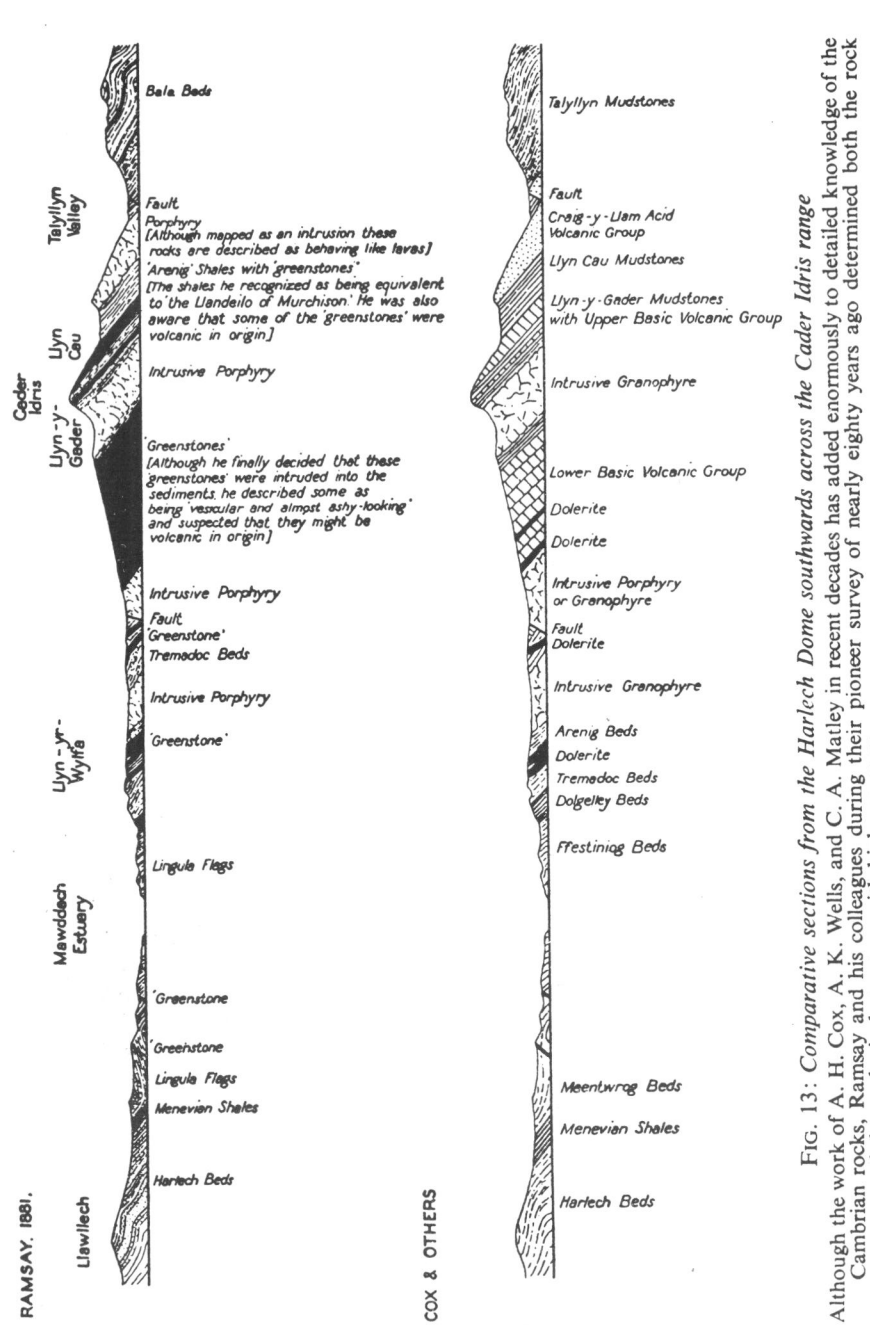

Fig. 13: *Comparative sections from the Harlech Dome southwards across the Cader Idris range*

Although the work of A. H. Cox, A. K. Wells, and C. A. Matley in recent decades has added enormously to detailed knowledge of the Cambrian rocks, Ramsay and his colleagues during their pioneer survey of nearly eighty years ago determined both the rock sequence and the geological structure with high accuracy.

Interstratified with the graptolitic beds of the higher part of the Arenig Series are some thin limestones (of which the *Ogygia* Limestone of the Arenig country is the most important) with a shelly fauna of trilobites and brachiopods, (including ' *Ogygia* ' *selwynii*, *Neseuretus* [*Calymene*] *parvifrons*, *Ampyx*, Orthids and *Lingula*). Slight vulcanicity is also indicated in the Arenig country by the occurrence of thin tuffs, the *Calymene* ' Ashes ', which, being submarine accumulations, contain a shelly fauna. These thicken southwards, and on Cader Idris the upper part of the Arenig Series consists of the ashes and rhyolitic lava flows of the Mynydd-y-Gader Volcanic Group, which reaches a thickness of over 1,000 ft.

LLANVIRN SERIES

Although in places coarse-grained, as in the Bryn Brith Grits of Cader Idris, the Llanvirn deposits mostly accumulated under relatively tranquil conditions and are similar lithologically to the *Tetragraptus* Shales of the upper part of the Arenig Series in consisting of mudstones and shales with a pelagic fauna of graptolites. The lower beds are characterized by *Didymograptus bifidus*, the upper by *D. murchisoni* (Fig. 12). They vary considerably in thickness, being negligibly developed about Rhobell Fawr, some 400 to 500 ft south of Dolgelley, and 1,500 to 1,600 ft in the Snowdon syncline (where, as the Maesgwm Slates, they were commercially worked at Blaenau Ffestiniog) and near Fairbourne. These variations in part reflect the effects of contemporary vulcanicity, for the sediments tend to be thickest where the extrusive rocks are relatively inconsiderable; but they may also be due to post-Llanvirn unconformity.

Llanvirn igneous activity was on an enormous scale. The outpourings form much of the Cader Idris range (Pl. VI, and Fig. 13), and although westwards they become thinner and less continuous, eastwards and northwards they can be followed in strength with their associated sediments around the Harlech Dome through the Arans, the Arenigs, and Migneint to the Manod and Moelwyn Hills.

On Arenig itself Fearnsides has described two separate series of volcanic rocks (Fig. 14). The lower lies at the top of the *Didymograptus bifidus* Shales and is largely fragmental in character, consisting of andesitic and rhyolitic tuffs and agglomerates which continue southwards and westwards into the Cader Idris range as the Cefn Hir Ashes: it has a thickness of 300 to 500 ft. The associated *D. bifidus* Shales, like the succeeding *D. murchisoni* Shales, contain many coarse sandy and gritty bands full of pyroclastic fragments. The upper series, resting on the *D. murchisoni* Shales and possibly of Llandeilo age, is also largely composed of andesitic and rhyolitic tuffs. Although reaching a thickness of over 4,000 ft in Arenig, it is not continued into the Cader Idris country, where, as Cox has shown, the upper part of the Llanvirn Series is marked by a separate group of volcanic rocks. These, extruded from a centre near Cader Idris, are local in their development, and are distinct both structurally and chemically from the rocks of Arenig. They constitute the Llyn-y-Gafr Group composed chiefly of some 1,500 ft of soda-rich spilitic lavas, often showing pillow forms: they contain many intercalations of ash and shale bands.

Rhyolites and andesites are the main constituents of the Manod (Lower Llanvirn) and Moelwyn (Upper Llanvirn) flows; and similar rocks, with some spilites, form the poorly exposed Rhiw Volcanic Series, of early Llanvirn age, of western Lleyn.

In Anglesey and in Snowdonia Llanvirn volcanic activity was negligible.

NORTH WALES

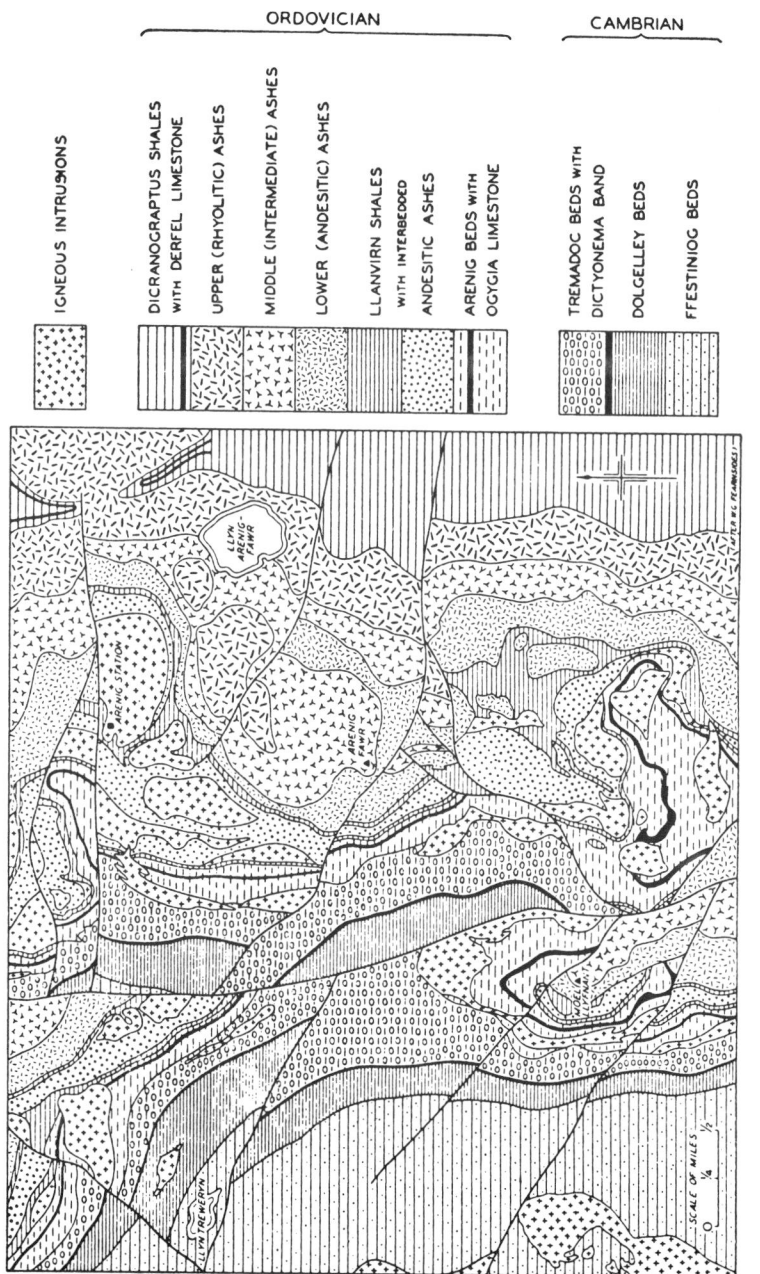

ORDOVICIAN | CAMBRIAN

IGNEOUS INTRUSIONS

DICRANOGRAPTUS SHALES WITH DERFEL LIMESTONE

UPPER (RHYOLITIC) ASHES

MIDDLE (INTERMEDIATE) ASHES

LOWER (ANDESITIC) ASHES

LLANVIRN SHALES WITH INTERBEDDED ANDESITIC ASHES

ARENIG BEDS WITH OGYGIA LIMESTONE

TREMADOC BEDS WITH DICTYONEMA BAND

DOLGELLEY BEDS

FFESTINIOG BEDS

Fig. 14: *Geological map of the Arenig country*

Llandeilo Series

Outside the Berwyn Hills it is doubtful if there are many localities in North Wales where sediments certainly referable to the Llandeilo Series (that is, the zone of *Glyptograptus teretiusculus*) have been recorded. In Anglesey and near Bangor, Greenly has included in the Series some 90 ft of shales which appear to follow on the *D. murchisoni* Shales in uninterrupted succession; but elsewhere

many so-called Llandeilo rocks may be the lower members of the Bala Series
—they belong to the zone of *Nemagraptus gracilis*, a graptolite species whose
range apparently overlaps the junction between the Llandeilo and the Bala Series.
It is possible that, as in the Arenig country and the Cader Idris range, the
absence of sediments is directly due to powerful volcanic activity that main-
tained the local land-surface above sea level throughout Llandeilo times.

   In the Berwyn Dome on the other hand the Llandeilo beds, possibly more
than 2,000 ft thick, were deposited in shallower water, or at least under more
normal neritic conditions, than the pelagic graptolitic shales and muds of the
north-western district: although usually fine-grained with many shale bands,
they present, especially in their lower layers, a contrasted lithological facies of
silts, sands, calcareous mudstones, and impure limestones in which graptolites
are rare (though *Glyptograptus teretiusculus* has been found) but shelly fossils
relatively common. The general nature of the rocks is very like that of the
Llandeilo Flags of the type area on the east flank of the Towy Anticline in South
Wales, and doubtless there was continuity of facies between the two areas.
Such trilobites as *Ogygiocarella [Ogygia] debuchii*, *Basilicus [Asaphus] tyrannus*,
and *Marrolithus [Trinucleus] favus*, and such brachiopods as *Dalmanella [Orthis]
rankini* and *Rafinesquina llandeiloensis*, are characteristic; they are found in
beds of Llandeilo Limestone in the lower part of the Series. Throughout the
succession there occur numerous bands of acid tuffs, and rarer lava flows: none of
them reaches any great thickness, and presumably they reflect only mild volcanic
activity, or their present outcrops lie at some distance from the source of
extrusion.

BALA (CARADOC AND ASHGILL) SERIES

   The probable absence of the Llandeilo Series over much of North Wales
implies that there were uplift, emergence, and erosion before the deposition of the
Bala Series. Direct evidence of the break is rarely visible, and only recently has the
application of graptolite zoning indicated its widespread occurrence in the stratigraphical proximity of the *D. bifidus*, *D. murchisoni* and *N. gracilis* zones. In
most localities there is a deceptive similarity of facies between the Lower Bala
and the Llanvirn beds; and only in Anglesey, where the *N. gracilis* Zone oversteps the Lower Ordovician to rest transgressively on the Pre-Cambrian (the
usual Bala shales following upon a very thick basal conglomerate with abundant
pebbles of Gwna quartzite), is there gross discordance. Nevertheless, the close
association, possibly along a fracture zone, of Bala and Upper Cambrian beds
in the neighbourhood of Tremadoc may be an acceptable sign of unconformity
of comparable magnitude on the mainland.

   In most of the western outcrops, from Snowdonia around the flanks of the
Harlech Dome, the characteristic development of the Lower Bala (Caradoc)
Series is one of grey mudstones and blue shales with thin siliceous bands, containing, though not abundantly, a graptolite fauna. In general they much
resemble the *Dicranograptus* Shales of South Wales, with which there was
continuity of sedimentation. In detail, however, they display considerable
variation.

   To the south and south-east of Dolgelley the Llyn-y-Gader and Llyn Cau
Mudstones are the basal members of the group which, as the Talyllyn Mudstones,
forms a thick series running north-eastwards to the Bala country. In the lowest
layers they contain fossils of the *N. gracilis* Zone, but the greater part of the

succession (the Ceiswyn Beds, reaching some 4,000 ft in total thickness) is almost unfossiliferous. From Corris through Llan-y-Mawddwy to Bala (where their equivalents are in part known as the Nant-hir Shales) the Ceiswyn Beds, described by Pugh, show appreciable lateral variation in lithology, mainly in the incoming of limestones and sandstones. On the flanks of Arenig, Fearnsides and Elles have proved the occurrence at or near the base of the *Dicranograptus* (Nant-hir) Shales of a richly fossiliferous impure limestone, the Derfel Limestone, with a shelly fauna, recently described by Whittington and Williams, of trilobites (including *Broeggerolithus* [*Trinucleus*] *harnagensis*, *Platylichas*, *Illaenus*, and *Harpes*) and brachiopods (including *Nicolella*, *Dolerothis*, *Platystrophia*, *Soudleyella avelinei*, *Horderleyella*, *Salopia salteri*, *Leptellina derfelensis*, and *Sowerbyella*): these forms, many of them new to Ordovician Britain, suggest (in complement to the sub-Bala unconformity) the opening of migration routes by radical change in contemporary geography. At the top of the Nant-hir Shales about Bala, Elles has described the occurrence of fossiliferous sandy beds: in ascending succession, with intercalated ash bands, these comprise the Glyn Gower Sandstones (which, with *Sowerbyella sericea*, may be the equivalent of part of the Meifod Sandstones, and of the Soudley Sandstone of Shropshire), the Allt-ddu Mudstones (with *Dinorthis flabellulum* and *Heterorthis alternata*), and the Gelli-Grin Ashes (with *Nicolella actoniae*). A similar succession is seen in the Berwyn Hills, where the Teirw Beds have been correlated with the Ceiswyn Beds and the Nant-hir Shales, and the Bryn Beds with the Glyn Gower Sandstone.

The topmost member of the Lower Bala Series near Machynlleth is the Nod Glas, a thin group of jet-black shales and mudstones with calcareous and phosphatic bands. In places it is richly fossiliferous with *Dicranograptus clingani* and a few graptolites which suggest also the presence of the higher zone of *Pleurograptus linearis* (though the zonal species has not been found). The equivalent beds in the Berwyn country are the Pen-y-garnedd Shales, the underlying Pen-y-garnedd Limestone containing *Nicolella actoniae*. The association of graptolitic muds with shelly limestones and phosphate deposits suggests deposition in tranquil but shallow-water lagoons.

The *Dicranograptus* Shales are represented by some 300 ft of shales and mudstones in Anglesey and 300 ft of shales (the Cadnant Shales) at Conway. Farther south they thicken to constitute the Glanrafon Slates, over 1,000 ft thick, of the Snowdon syncline. About Snowdon itself these beds merge upwards into a greywacke suite, the Gwastadnant Grits, a group that, with interbedded shales, reaches nearly 2,000 ft south-westwards in the neighbourhood of Moel Hebog, but that is not readily recognised north-east towards Dolwyddelan and the Conway Valley, where the sediments become progressively finer in grain—a relationship that suggests derivation of the grits from a western or north-western source. The grits in places contain a shelly fauna with *Broeggerolithus* [*Trinucleus*] *harnagensis*, *Parabasilicus* [*Asaphus*] *powisii*, *Dinorthis flabellulum*, and *Sowerbyella soudleyensis*. The Snowdon Volcanic Series interrupts the sedimentary succession above the Glanrafon Slates; but resting immediately on the uppermost rhyolites, both at Dolwyddelan and Trefriw, are black graptolitic shales lithologically like the Nod Glas and some of the Cadnant Shales.

The Upper Bala (Ashgill) Series displays changes broadly similar to those of the Caradoc. In the Corris district south-west of Cader Idris is a great thickness (nearly 5,000 ft locally) of mudstones and shales, often cleaved, containing a sparse fauna of graptolites: the lower part, the Abercwmeiddaw Group (1,600 ft),

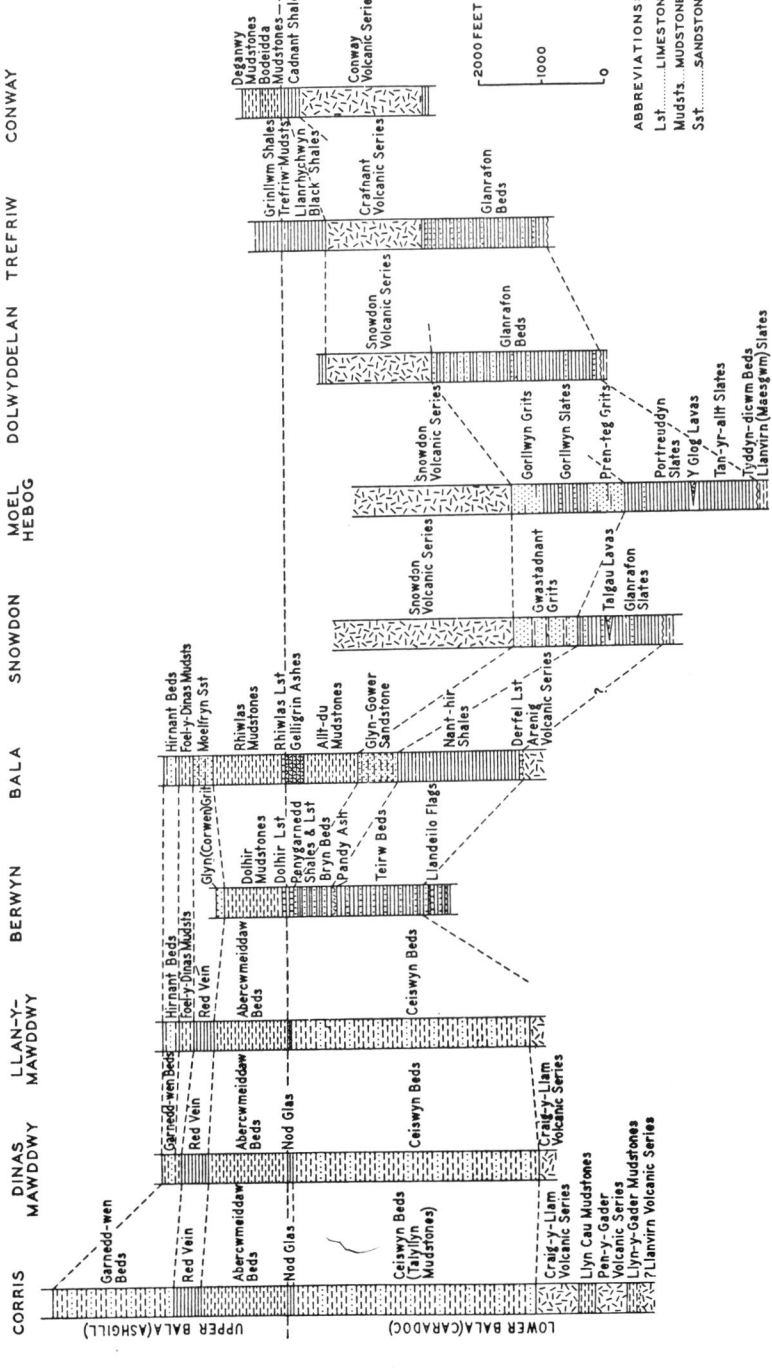

FIG. 15: *Comparative sections showing lateral changes in the Bala Series of North Wales*

The lines of correlation are in places only approximate: in particular, the range of volcanic activity was almost certainly not uniform from one locality to another.

is pale grey with dark mottling, and has yielded *Orthograptus truncatus* and *Dicellograptus anceps*; the upper, the Garnedd-wen Beds (3,000 ft at maximum), is dark-blue, rusty-weathering, mostly unfossiliferous. Towards the north-east, as Elles and Pugh have shown, an unconformity is developed at the base of the series, which becomes very much thinner (some 2,000 ft in total) and near Bala includes many calcareous and sandy beds with a dominantly shelly fauna. The Abercwmeiddaw Group passes laterally into the Rhiwlas Mudstones (with beds of ' Bala ' limestones), containing *Dicellograptus anceps* and *Phillipsinella parabola*, its uppermost member, the Red Vein, becoming the Moelfryn Sandstone; the lower Garnedd-wen Beds pass into the Foel-y-Dinas Mudstones, with *Dalmanitina* [*Phacops*] *mucronata*; and the upper Garnedd-wen Beds into the Hirnant Shales, with *Stropheodonta* (*Eostropheodonta*) *hirnantensis*. Without any apparent non-sequence developing, the 3,000 ft of Garnedd-wen Beds near Corris are reduced to only a few hundred feet of calcareous mudstones between Llan-y-Mawddwy and Bala. A sequence very similar to that at Bala is found in the Berwyn Hills, where the Dolhir Mudstones are the equivalent of the Rhiwlas and the Glyn or Corwen Grit of the Moelfryn Sandstone. At Conway also the calcareous mudstone facies is dominant, the successive Bodeidda and Deganwy Mudstones (about 600 ft together) yielding Orthids and trilobites (including *Phillipsinella parabola*).

Rocks of Upper Bala age are not known in Anglesey or Snowdonia.

In general, therefore, the Bala Series provides evidence of maximum sedimentation to the west (with greywackes) and to the south-west (with unfossiliferous mudstones). In the north and north-west, graptolitic shales are dominant. To the east and north-east neritic sediments of shelf-sea type become increasingly important, with a much more varied and abundant shelly fauna (see Fig. 15).

In places, particularly in the neighbourhood of Corris and Dinas Mawddwy, the Bala shales and mudstones were cleaved by the Caledonian movements to form slates that have been quarried on an extensive scale.

THE BALA VOLCANIC SERIES

During Lower Bala times volcanoes erupted from a number of centres mainly situated in Caernarvonshire, where their products form the Bala Volcanic Series. Early in the epoch they became active somewhere in the neighbourhood of Conway, and rhyolites and rhyolitic tuffs were poured out in great quantity over an extensive area from Conway to Ffestiniog. These rocks were approximately contemporaneous with rhyolites poured from a vent situated in the hills behind Bethesda and Capel Curig, though the Capel Curig suite, 1,500 ft thick, is not so thick as the Conway Series, 2,500 ft. In the Cader Idris country the spilitic pillow lavas of the Pen-y-Gader Volcanic Group, underlying the Llyn Cau Mudstones, are of much the same age, though not of the same origin, while slightly younger, overlying the Mudstones, are the rhyolites and andesites, 1,200 ft thick, of the Craig-y-Llam Group. Interdigitating with the flows of the Conway Series, the Crafnant Series, also of rhyolites and rhyolitic tuffs, covers an extensive tract to the west of Llanrwst.

The Snowdon Series, slightly later in age, gives rise to the rugged scenery of much of Snowdonia (Pls. I, VII, and X). It is largely derived from vents in the neighbourhood of Snowdon itself, though it is probable that eruptions occurred sporadically from a number of aligned vents trending in a north-east and south-

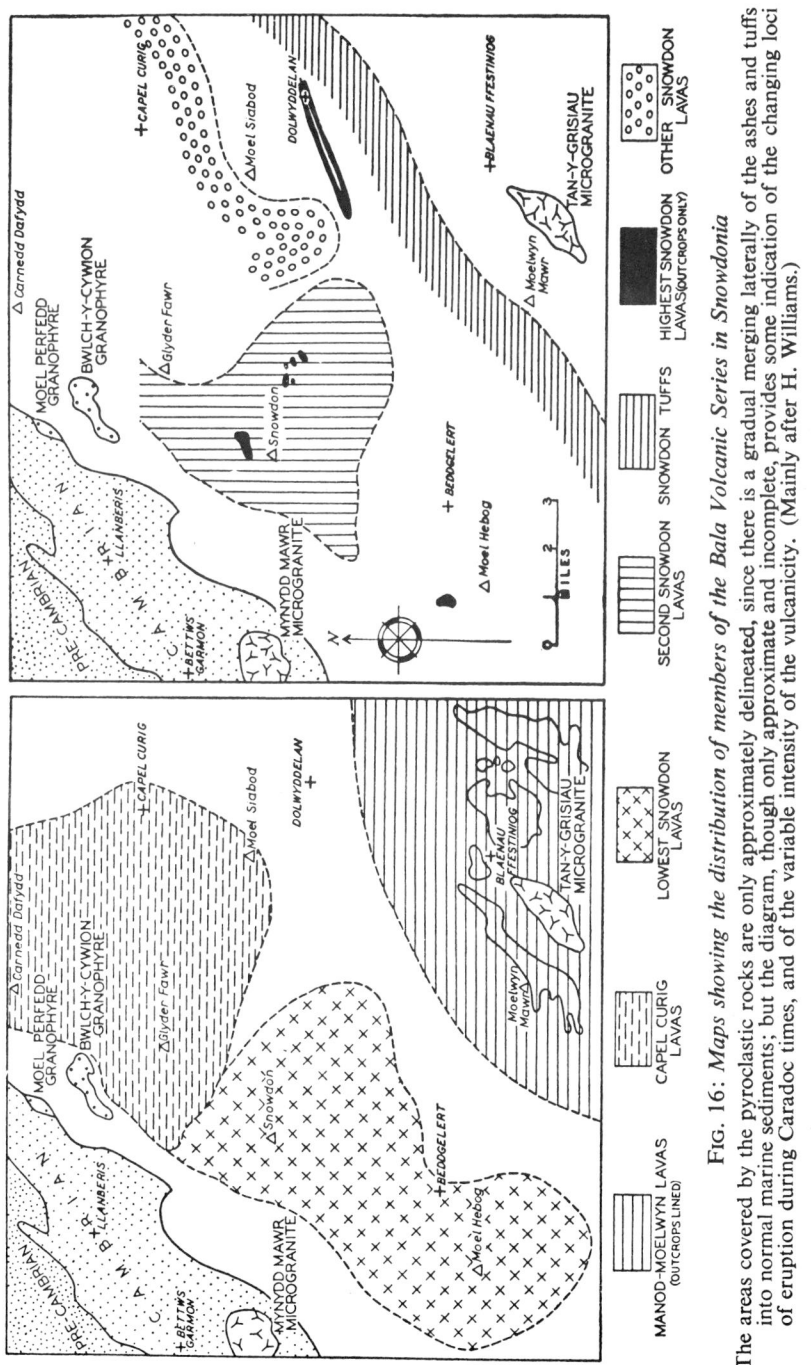

Fig. 16: *Maps showing the distribution of members of the Bala Volcanic Series in Snowdonia*

The areas covered by the pyroclastic rocks are only approximately delineated, since there is a gradual merging laterally of the ashes and tuffs into normal marine sediments; but the diagram, though only approximate and incomplete, provides some indication of the changing loci of eruption during Caradoc times, and of the variable intensity of the vulcanicity. (Mainly after H. Williams.)

west direction from Conway towards Pwllheli. Contemporaneous lavas and tuffs are thickly developed on Moel Hebog and Llwyd Mawr (Fig. 16). The volcanic rocks of the central part of the Snowdon syncline are nearly all of acid rhyolitic composition. Introduced by thin rhyolites in the Glanrafon Beds and Gwastadnant Grits, they have been divided by H. and D. Williams into two groups of rhyolites and rhyolitic tuffs, totalling nearly 2,000 ft, whose formation was separated by a period of relative quiescence when fossiliferous sediments were interbedded with stratified pyroclastic fragmental rocks (Fig. 17). Soda-rich spilites, keratophyres, and andesites, erupted from local centres, have also been recognised by Matley in the Caradoc Series at a number of localities in Lleyn. Shackleton has shown that the same broad sequence continues into Moel Hebog.

Similar acidic ashes and tuffs occur as thin bands in the sandy Bala mudstones of the Berwyn Hills, the chief of which are the Cwmclwyd Ash (Pl. VB), 150 ft thick, and the Pandy Ash, 60 ft thick.

All the volcanoes had become quiescent, if not quite extinct, by the beginning of Ashgill times.

IGNEOUS INTRUSIONS

Associated with the extrusive lavas, ashes, and tuffs, very many igneous intrusions of pre-Silurian age cut through the Ordovician sediments. The larger often form at the present day steep isolated hills (Pl. VIIIB), and are probably in many cases the plugs of the ancient volcanoes.

In number most of these intrusive rocks are of basic types, chiefly doleritic dykes; they include quartz-dolerites and (near Aberdaron) albite-dolerites. As in the case of the Mynydd-y-Gader intrusion near Dolgelley and of some of the andesitic dolerites of Arenig Fawr, they are probably not much younger than the volcanic rocks with which they are associated.

The acid intrusions, though of more restricted occurrence, are generally larger in size. They are mostly of granitic and porphyritic types: examples include the Bwlch-y-Cywion granite and granophyre, the riebeckite microgranite of Mynydd Mawr, and the porphyries of Drosgl, Penmaenmawr, Nevin, and Llanbedrog. Davies has recently shown that the granophyre dominating the face of the scarp of Cader Idris (Pl. VIA) was intruded at a late stage in the eruption of the Craig-y-Llam Volcanic Series, apophyses probably being vent-feeders of the uppermost lavas; and that its emplacement lifted its roof (of rocks about 2,000 ft in thickness) some 1,500 ft in places, well above neighbouring sea level.

The mineralisation of the Lower Palaeozoic rocks of North Wales (including the Dolgelley gold belt) is for the most part to be attributed to deep-seated solutions associated with these Ordovician igneous intrusions (see p. 24).

PISOLITIC ORES

Oolitic and pisolitic iron ores are interbedded with marine sediments at various horizons from Upper Cambrian to Middle Ordovician and are found at a number of localities in Caernarvonshire, Merioneth, and Anglesey.

The ore bodies as a rule are of small extent and thickness, occurring as lenticles or as beds drawn out by earth movements. They consist mainly of chlorite with or without clastic constituents, and locally peculiar varieties contain

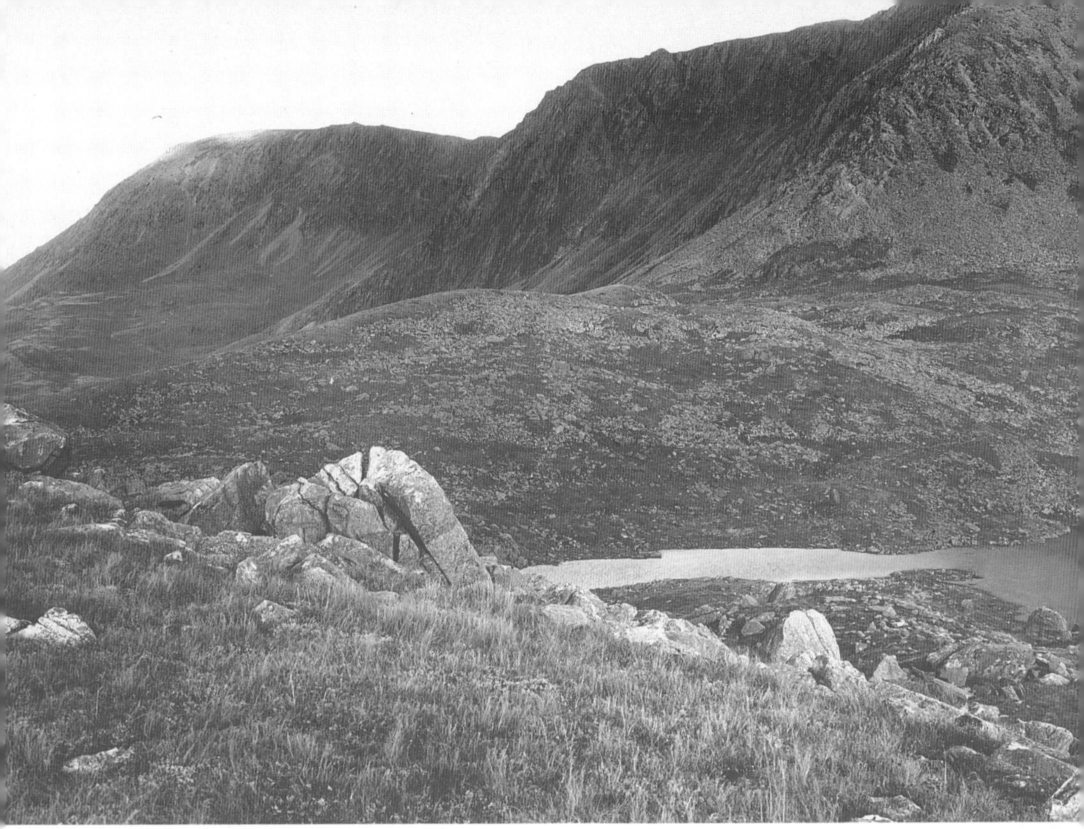

(A.6517)

A. The face of the Cader Idris escarpment

Plate VI

B. Graig Llwyd quarries, Penmaenmawr

(*Cambridge Univ. Collection: copyright reserved*)

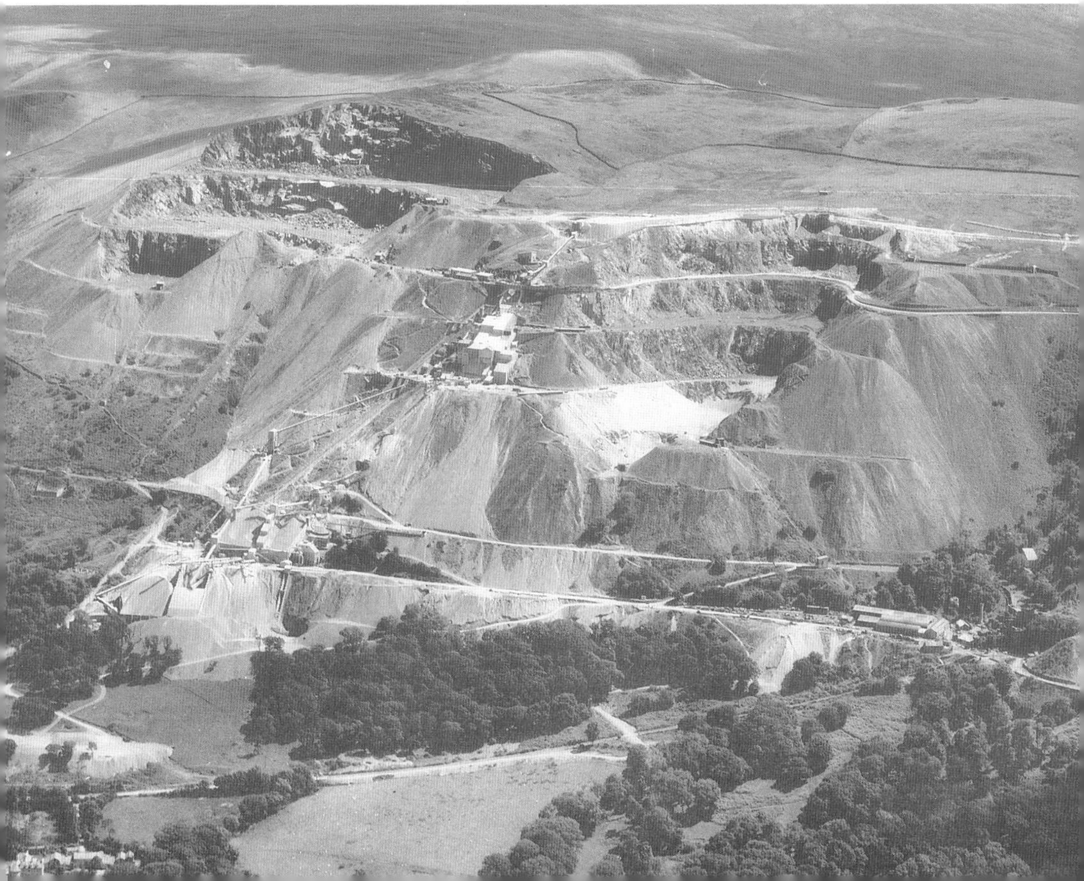

(A.6486)

A. The Pass of Llanberis

Plate VII

B. Snowdon from near Llanberis

(A.6496)

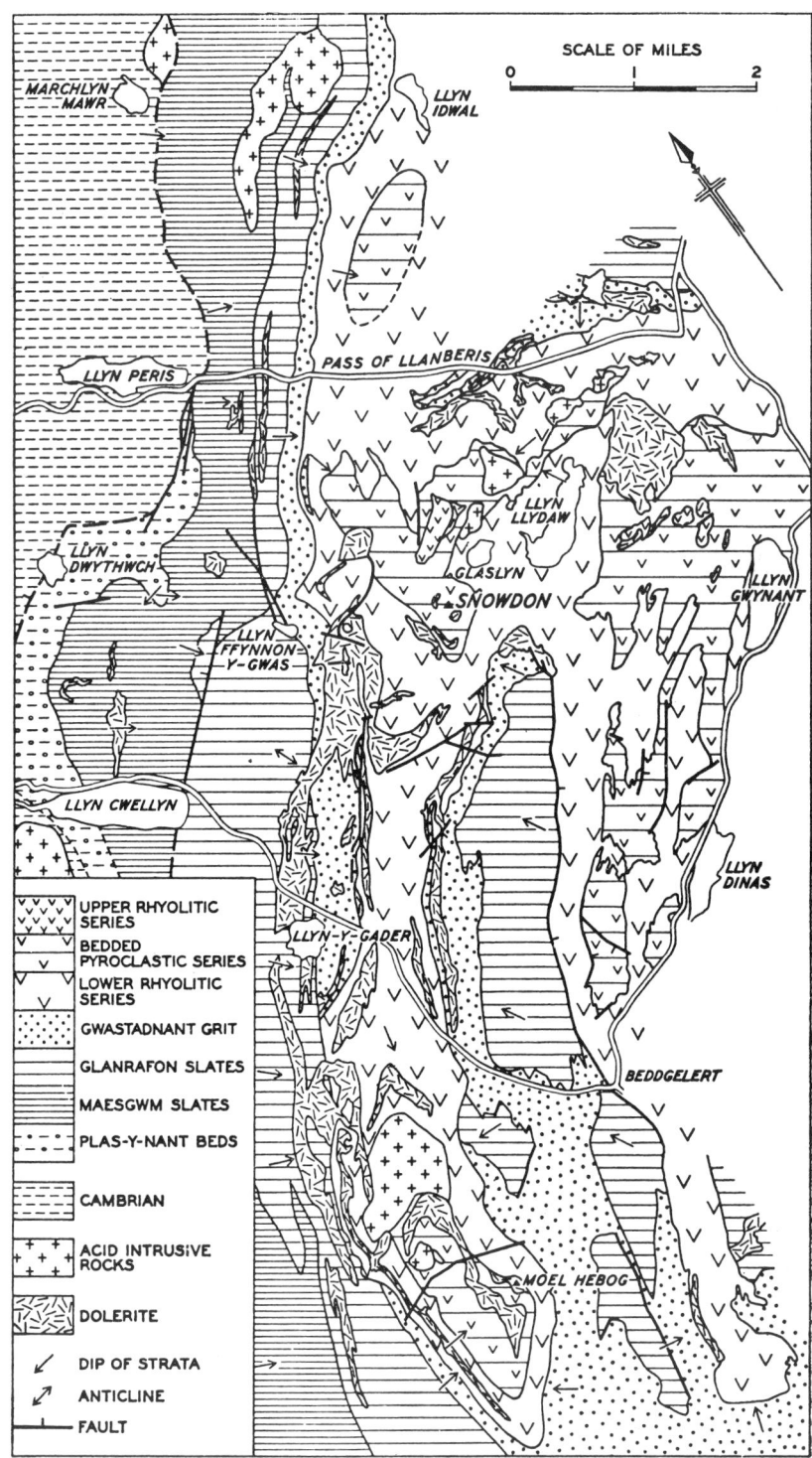

SCALE OF MILES
0   1   2

MARCHLYN-MAWR

LLYN IDWAL

PASS OF LLANBERIS

LLYN PERIS

LLYN LLYDAW

LLYN DWYTHWCH

GLASLYN

SNOWDON

LLYN GWYNANT

LLYN FFYNNON-Y-GWAS

LLYN CWELLYN

LLYN DINAS

LLYN-Y-GADER

BEDDGELERT

MOEL HEBOG

UPPER RHYOLITIC SERIES

BEDDED PYROCLASTIC SERIES

LOWER RHYOLITIC SERIES

GWASTADNANT GRIT

GLANRAFON SLATES

MAESGWM SLATES

PLAS-Y-NANT BEDS

CAMBRIAN

ACID INTRUSIVE ROCKS

DOLERITE

DIP OF STRATA

ANTICLINE

FAULT

FIG. 17: *Geological map of the Snowdon district*
(Slightly simplified, after H. Williams, D. Williams, and R. M. Shackleton.)

haematite, pyrite, and siderite, usually associated with chlorite. They generally contain nodules bearing sponge spicules.

According to Pulfrey, most of the ooliths grew *in situ* in the consolidating rocks, which were deposited on an uneven surface in a sub-coastal region, and were invariably succeeded by sediments indicating quiet deposition of fine-grained detritus.

The best known ore bodies occur at Bettws Garmon, of Upper Cambrian age, and at Cader Idris, Llanengan (St. Tudwal's Peninsula), Tremadoc, Trefriw, and Anglesey, all of which are of Caradoc age, as probably is that of Llandegai near Bangor.

Manganese ores showing oolitic and pisolitic structures occur in the Arenig rocks of Lleyn. Described by Woodland and Groves, they appear to have originated under the influence of manganese solutions (perhaps migrating from volcanic sources) by the alteration in part of chamositic mudstones, in part of keratophyric tuff. The rocks were broken into strips and lenticles by thrusting and shearing, and economic exploitation of the ore is correspondingly difficult.

V. THE SILURIAN SYSTEM

SILURIAN ROCKS occupy extensive tracts of North Wales, being found over the greater part of the Denbighshire Moors, in the Clwydian Range, in the Llangollen syncline between the Ordovician rocks of the Berwyns and of Mynydd Cricor, and along a belt, the Central Wales syncline, that widens southwards from Mynydd Bwlch-y-groes near Bala into the highlands of Central Wales about Plynlimon.

The Silurian sediments show much variation in lithology, and were affected by slight earth-movements recurrent from late Ordovician times. In the eastern part of the area, notably on the southern flank of the Berwyn anticline, elevation and emergence of the sea floor are reflected in a visible unconformity between the Silurian rocks and the underlying Bala Series, and coarse sandy and conglomeratic beds indicate strong erosion of a nearby coast. Elsewhere, however, fine-grained sediments continued uninterruptedly (though sometimes with sharp colour-differences) across the junction between the Ordovician system and the Silurian, and much of North Wales was covered by Lower Palaeozoic seas from the Bala transgression until the final Silurian retreat. In regional development the broad distribution of land and sea thus remained little changed as Ordovician times passed into Silurian: the local frame of the geosyncline was marked by a shore or shelf line nearby to the south-east, probably in the neighbourhood of the Church Stretton fault in Shropshire, that fluctuated in position in response to the accidents of pulsatory subsidence; and by deeper troughs to the north-west where sedimentation was continuous. In one important particular, however, the Silurian rocks of North Wales differ from the Ordovician: they show no sign of contemporary volcanic action, and the declining eruptions of later Bala times were followed by complete extinction.

Like the Ordovician, the Silurian rocks reflect geosynclinal conditions and three main rock facies can be recognized: (i) a pelagic or lagoonal facies of shales and mudstones typically with layers rich in graptolites, (ii) a 'foredeep' facies of coarse thick greywackes often showing signs of transport by turbidity currents, and (iii) a shallow-water neritic facies of sands, silts, mudstones, and limestones usually with a shelly fauna of trilobites, brachiopods, molluscs, and corals (see Fig. 18). The three facies are well exemplified by the earlier Silurian rocks, but the distinctions tend to break down in the later mainly in a rarity or absence of true blue-black graptolitic shales. They were finally obliterated completely when at the close of Silurian times the Lower Palaeozoic seas retreated from North Wales, the geosynclinal frame of sedimentation was destroyed, strong earth-movements transformed the landscape, and the marine rocks of the Cambrian, Ordovician, and Silurian systems were replaced by the continental rocks of the Old Red Sandstone.

The Silurian rocks may be divided into three series, which, originally established in the Welsh Border country on a lithological basis, are now recognized by means of their fossils. These are:

3. LUDLOW SERIES. The characteristic graptolites of this series are of the type of *Monograptus nilssoni*, *M. scanicus*, *M. tumescens*, and *M. leintwardinensis*, which possess relatively simple thecae and are forms in evolutionary decline. In the middle part of the series the graptolites become rarer and finally

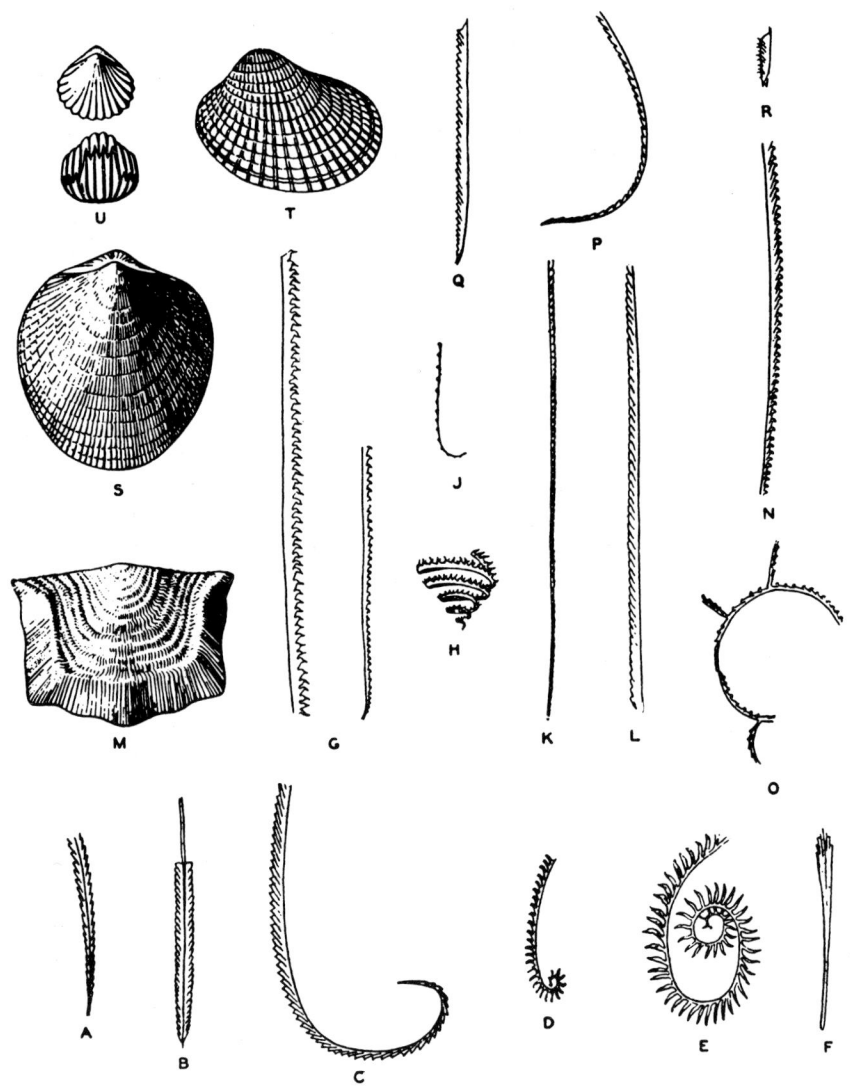

FIG. 18: *Silurian fossils*

(All natural size; graptolite drawings after Elles and Wood).

Lower Llandovery Series, **A,** *Akidograptus [Cephalograptus] acuminatus* (Nicholson); **B,** *Diplo-graptus [Mesograptus] modestus* Lapworth; **C,** *Monograptus cyphus* Lapworth; **D,** *M. triangulatus* (Harkness); **E,** *M. convolutus* (Hisinger); **F,** *Cephalograptus cometa* (Geinitz). Upper Llandovery Series, **G,** *Monograptus sedgwickii* (Portlock); **H,** *M. turriculatus* (Barrande); **J,** *M. crispus* Lapworth; **K,** *M. griestoniensis* (Nicol); **L,** *M. crenulatus* Törnquist; **M,** *Leptaena rhomboidalis* (Wilckens). Wenlock Series, **N,** *Monograptus riccartonensis* Lapworth; **O,** *Cyrtograptus lundgreni* Tullberg. Ludlow Series, **P,** *M. nilssoni* (Barrande); **Q,** *M. tumescens* Wood; **R,** *M. leintwardinensis* Lapworth; **S,** *Atrypa reticularis* (Linnaeus); **T,** *Slava interrupta* J. de C. Sowerby; **U,** *Camarotoechia nucula* (J. de C. Sowerby).

completely absent. Their extinction is probably to be correlated with the change in physical conditions that prefaced the breakdown of the geosyncline and the advent of the sub-continental beds of the Devonian Downton Series.

2. WENLOCK SERIES. The characteristic graptolites are *Cyrtograptus* and forms like *Monograptus riccartonensis*.

1. VALENTIAN or LLANDOVERY SERIES. The graptolite fauna is mixed, and includes species of persistent Ordovician biserial genera (*Diplograptus, Glyptograptus*) together with transitional forms (*Dimorphograptus*) and new Silurian arrivals: chief amongst the latter are rapidly evolving Monograptid species that developed elaborate thecae, including *Monograptus sedgwickii*, *M. priodon*, *M. crispus*, *M. triangulatus*, *M. convolutus*, *M. crenulatus*, and *Rastrites*.

VALENTIAN SERIES

In North Wales the rocks of the Valentian Series fall into the two broad groups that have been recognized in the type areas to the south: (i) a group (the Llandovery facies) of variable lithology with a shelly fauna of brachiopods and trilobites; and (ii) a group (the Tarannon facies) of pale grey, green, and purple shales generally with an almost exclusively graptolitic fauna. In many places beds of Tarannon type follow beds of Llandovery type—a consequence of the regional deepening that followed the minor earth-movements at the close of Ordovician times—and for long it was thought that the two divisions were in true stratigraphical order. It is now known, however, that the change from one rock-type to the other did not take place everywhere at the same time, and a simple classification of the deposits on a facies basis is at variance with a chronological classification based on the succession of graptolite zones: that is, the individual facies belts transgress the time planes. Llandovery-type rocks may locally span the whole time-interval of the series, and the place-name has now come to be used for the whole group of strata as a chronological term applicable to every kind of facies. The term Tarannon on the other hand is limited to the graptolite shale facies of Upper Valentian age.

Along the western and south-western outcrops, from Conway through the Bala country towards Llan-y-Mawddwy and Machynlleth, the whole of the Valentian Series consists of blue, black, and grey graptolitic shales and mudstones with only occasional interbedded sandy and gritty bands. The Gyffin Shales of the Conway district were probably near the axial trough of the geosyncline: Elles has described them as exceedingly fine-grained rocks which must have accumulated very slowly, for although they are only 300 ft thick they contain all the graptolite zones and were deposited without break. Very similar black graptolitic shales have also been found in the Parys Mountain district of Anglesey. Between Llan-y-Mawddwy and Corris, in ground described by Pugh, the Lower and Middle Valentian rocks (the Pont Erwyd stage) are some 400 to 500 ft thick: but although thicker than the Conway development their lithology continues to be essentially argillaceous, consisting of striped blue mudstones and cleaved shales with a graptolitic fauna. The Upper Valentian rocks (the Ystwyth stage) on the other hand show notable changes: they increase in thickness from about 1,000 ft near Llanuwchllyn to about 2,000 ft near Machynlleth and Talerddig, where Bassett has shown the group to display high variability in elements of thickness and lithology, and to contain representatives of the Talerddig Grits that thicken south-westwards. The evidence is of irregular deposition in an environment disturbed by turbidity currents and perhaps by submarine flows carrying muds unequally distributed. The Ystwyth stage finally reaches 8,000 ft on the flanks of Plynlimon a few miles beyond the North Wales area—an increase partly due to thickening lenses of arenaceous sediments, first as ribs of sandstone and grit but south of Machynlleth as massive greywackes with conglomeratic layers. These coarse-grained sediments are generally ill-sorted, and their lithology and thickness suggest accumulation in a foredeep of the geosyncline: the occurrence of graptolitic layers in the inter-bedded shales is strong evidence against their being truly shallow-water deposits. The greywackes and grits thicken, and appear at successively lower horizons in the sequence, as they are followed from Montgomeryshire into Cardiganshire, and it is to be inferred that their detritus was derived from a land-mass lying to the west or south-west of the present outcrops in Central Wales.

The Valentian rocks that nowadays crop out along the flanks of the Llangollen syncline bear some lithological resemblance to those of the Llan-y-Mawddwy district; but the mudstones are often silty or even sandy, and were probably deposited towards the peripheral shallows of the geosyncline, for the arenaceous beds tend to be well sorted and not of greywacke type. At the same time, the slight coarsening of grain is accompanied by modifications in the fossil assem-blages in both the Lower and Middle and the Upper Valentian stages; and although bands of graptolitic shale permit correlation with the south-western outcrops, the mudstones contain a mixed fauna of trilobites (*Acidaspis, Phacops elegans, Portlockia [Phacops] stokesii*), brachiopods (Orthids, Pentamerids, *Sowerbyella, Leptaena, Atrypa, Meristina*), and corals (*Favosites*). There is considerable variation in thickness, the reasons for which are not obvious, though in part it is due to slight contemporaneous movements and intraformational non-sequences. Thus at Llansantffraid-Glyn-Ceiriog the Valentian Series is only 250 ft thick, a number of the upper zones of the Lower Valentian being overstepped; while northwards and north-westwards about Moel Ferna and Corwen it reaches 600 ft, and on the northern flank of the syncline around Mynydd Cricor and Cyrn-y-brain about 1,800 ft thick.

On the southern slopes of the Berwyns near Llanfyllin the Valentian rocks are also thin—not much more than 400 ft—but the thinning does not seem to be due to non-sequence. The almost complete absence of graptolite bands, however, makes precise correlation difficult, and the detailed zonal sequence is not known with certainty. The series rests unconformably on the Ashgill Beds over the greater part of its outcrop.

Farther south, in the Meifod district, King has shown the Series to thicken to about 1,000 ft, of which some 650 ft of blue silty mudstones with a basal sandstone are mainly Lower and Middle Valentian in age, and 330 ft of pale grey and purple shales of Tarannon type are Upper Valentian. A few graptolites (*Climacograptus normalis, Monograptus acinaces*) have been found in the Lower Valentian rocks, but the dominant fossils are trilobites and brachiopods and include *Phacops spp., Encrinurus punctatus*, Orthids, *Clorinda [Pentamerus] undata, Stricklandia lens, Leptaena, Plectodonta, Atrypa, Meristina crassa, Camarotoechia*, and the corals *Favosites* and *Halysites. Monograptus crispus, M. priodon, M. crenulatus*, and *Rastrites* are common in the Upper Valentian rocks, but there also occur *Phacops elegans* and other trilobites, and brachiopods. In parts of this area, Whittington has recorded post-Ordovician uplift and erosion to be so considerable that the Valentian Series oversteps the Ashgillian to rest on the Caradocian: the earliest Valentian sediments are correspondingly coarse sub-littoral sandstones (the Craigwen Sandstone), sandy limestones, and con-glomeratic grits resting in the hollows of the underlying eroded Ordovician floor.

Near Welshpool, still farther to the south-east, the Valentian succession is incomplete through overlap, the ground having been sufficiently elevated at the end of Ordovician times to remain above the level of the transgressive Silurian sea until later Lower Valentian times. In consequence the uppermost Ordovician strata suffered erosion, and, as in the Meifod-Llansantffraid country, the Ashgill Beds are completely overstepped in places and the local Valentian base

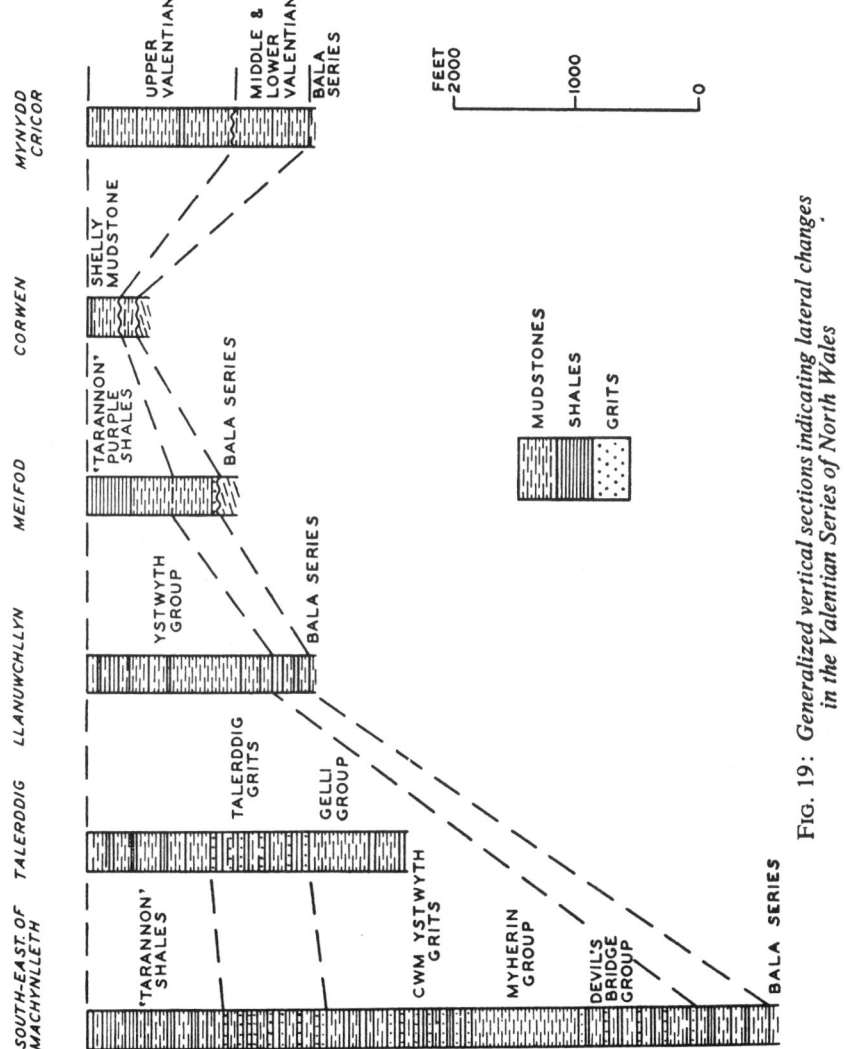

FIG. 19: Generalized vertical sections indicating lateral changes in the Valentian Series of North Wales

crosses on to rocks of Caradoc age. The evidence is thus conclusive that in earliest Silurian times the south-eastern margin of the geosyncline ran through this ground. The Valentian basement beds consist of very coarse grits and sandstones overlying a basal conglomerate that Wade, following Murchison, has called the Powys Castle Conglomerate. They are followed by flags and mudstones with a shelly fauna (including *Pentamerus oblongus*), which in turn are overlain by the purple Buttington Shales of Tarannon type (though they are almost completely barren of graptolites).

WENLOCK SERIES

The Wenlock and Ludlow Series are together united as the Salopian; and over much of North Wales the separation of the two, dependent on the detailed mapping of the graptolite zones, has not yet been effected (though it is not likely to be difficult). The rocks of both series are lithologically members of the same broad facies, and consist of mudstones and shales alternating with flags, sandstones and grits.

The Wenlock Series, defined by the association of *Monograptus* and *Cyrtograptus* without *Diplograptus*, is found in outcrops flanking the syncline of the Denbighshire Moors along the Conway Valley and thence continuing eastward to Mynydd Cricor and Cyrn-y-brain. It forms the axial belt of the Central Wales syncline from near Corwen southwards beyond Lake Vyrnwy, and of the subsidiary synclines running south-westwards about Llanfyllin and Welshpool. It floors wide expanses of country in the moorlands of Central Wales west of Newtown and Montgomery. Over such a wide area it displays notable changes of facies, which throw light on conditions of deposition.

The western facies is well displayed in the neighbourhood of Conway, where it comprises a succession of finely cross-bedded shales and coarse sandstones, frequently conglomeratic, that have been called by Elles the Benarth Grits and Flags. This lithological type is continued to the east and south as a series of alternating grits and shales, reaching a thickness of 4,000 ft in places, that form the Denbighshire Grits of the Denbighshire Moors, described by Boswell. The coarser sediments tend to be impersistent, the harder beds eroding to surface scarplets running for a few hundred yards and then being replaced by scarplets at higher or lower horizons. Occasional graptolites (including *Cyrtograptus*) are found in the shales; but the mudstones and sandstones usually contain a shelly fauna, sometimes with corals and crinoids. Farther south, in the Central Wales syncline between Bala and the Berwyn Dome, the Wenlock grits again form conspicuous features in the succession, and account for some of the rugged and picturesque scenery about Lake Vyrnwy. In these outcrops the encroachment of the coarse greywackes into ground earlier occupied by fine-grained graptolitic Tarannon shales marks a major change in palaeogeography; and notable shallowing must have occurred in post-Valentian times. In places the shallowing was the result of positive uplift accompanied by erosion and unconformity, for the Wenlock beds overstep the Valentian and come to rest on Ordovician rocks, for instance near Llanrwst and near Llanfair-Caereinion.

The variable development of the grits and greywackes results in enormous variations in thickness. In the neighbourhood of Colwyn Bay, where coarse sediments are almost completely absent (though siltstones and fine flaggy beds occur), the Wenlock Series is little over 1,000 ft thick; but at Llanrwst, ten miles to the south, over 2,000 ft of ribbon-banded flags with massive grits contribute to a total thickness approaching 4,000 ft. Similarly on the eastern flank of the Denbighshire Moors, a development of nearly 4,000 ft of flags and sandstones with conglomerates contrasts with less than 300 ft of slates and mudstones in the ground between Llangollen and Corwen. Moreover, as Cummins has pointed out, the first influx of grits was relatively early in the southern part of the outcrop west of Llanfyllin, relatively late farther north about Corwen and in the Conway valley. On the other hand, cessation of grit deposition in the North Wales area was more or less synchronous, and everywhere the uppermost Wenlock beds are fine-grained mudstones and shales.

Many of the coarser sediments display graded bedding, and ill-sorted grey-wackes bear such linear structures on their surface as flute casts, groove-casts and current ripples; and since they alternate with undisturbed finely laminated mud-stones and shales, Cummins has inferred that they were transported by spasmodic turbidity currents, the aligned sedimentary structures and the distribution of the coarser beds indicating movement from, and a source of sediment towards, the south-west or south (see Fig. 20).

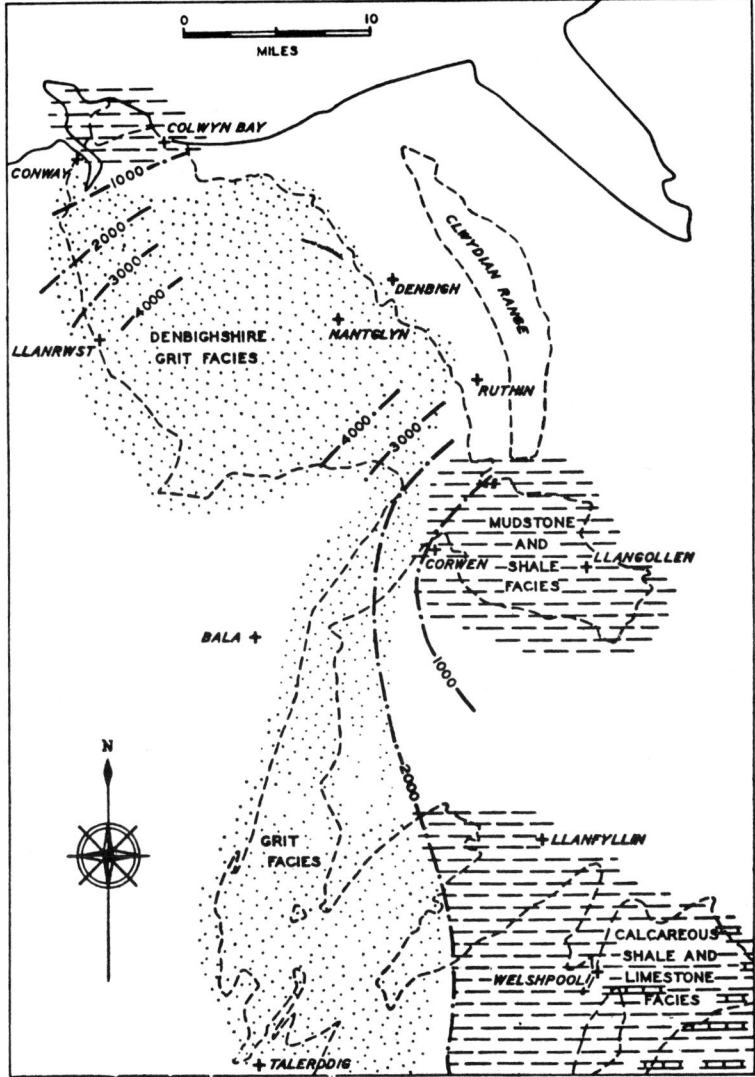

FIG. 20: *Facies and isopach map of the Wenlock Series in North Wales*

There is a merging of facies, and layers of grit occur in the dominantly shale and mudstone facies. Even when the Denbighshire Grits are at maximum development they contain mudstone intercalations, and everywhere are overlain by several hundred feet of mud-stones. The isopachs shown in 1000-ft intervals are partly conjectural. The outcrops of Silurian rocks are indicated by a broken line. (In part after Cummins.)

At no great distance away from the area of greywacke sedimentation, in the Severn valley about Welshpool, a third major facies makes a relatively abrupt onset to the south-east. It consists of an association of shales and fine flags, often calcareous, with impure concretionary limestones that are the first signs in North Wales of the kinds of sediments typical of the Wenlock Shales of Shropshire. Unlike the sands and grits of the subsidiary basin to the north and west, they are characteristic shallow-water rocks of a neritic shelf; and they contain common fossils of a great variety, including trilobites (*Dalmanites caudatus, Portlockia stokesii, Calymene blumenbachii*), brachiopods (*Leptaena rhomboidalis, Resserella [Orthis] elegantula, Eospirifer radiatus, Atrypa reticularis*), molluscs, polyzoans and corals.

LUDLOW SERIES

The Ludlow beds have a more limited distribution than the Wenlock: they are confined to the Denbighshire and Llangollen synclines and the Clwydian range, and to a tongue of the Central Wales syncline closing northwards near Lake Vyrnwy.

At all localities in North Wales where the junction is clearly exposed, the Ludlow Series follows the Wenlock with conformity, often with undefined lithological transition, and the distinction between them rests upon differences in the graptolitic faunas, particularly in the absence from the Ludlow of species of *Cyrtograptus*. In general lithology also there is close similarity between the Ludlow beds and the Wenlock, though the facies of the massive Denbighshire Grits is not strongly developed higher in the sequence than the middle part of the Wenlock. From the Conway valley to the Llangollen district the Ludlow Series displays a general uniformity, and consists of a succession, 4,500–5,000 ft in residual thickness, of mudstones, siltstones, and flags, with beds of sandstone.

The earliest member is the Nantglyn Flags, a group of rocks continuing from the upper Wenlock a type of sedimentation characterized by laminated or ribbon-banded alternations of mudstones, muddy siltstones, and calcareous siltstones. Graptolites are common on some of the bedding planes, but shelly fossils— nautiloids, starfishes, molluscs (notably *Slava interrupta*), brachiopods (*Dayia navicula, Sphaerirhynchia wilsoni, Chonetoidea grayi, 'Chonetes' laevigatus*), trilobites, and crinoids (notably large and sometimes perfectly preserved specimens of *Periechocrinus [Actinocrinus] pulcher*)—are also present and there is no clearly defined distinction between a graptolitic and a shelly facies. Most of the mudstones are unbrokenly finely laminated, but they and many of the siltstones may have a mottled appearance due to the primary bedding having been disturbed by mud-burrowing scavengers. Some of the more calcareous layers show such sedimentary structures as graded bedding, contorted bedding, flute casts, and aligned swarms of graptolites that are signs of sedimentation by fast-flowing currents, and, as Cummins has suggested, they may be turbidites.

Above the Nantglyn Flags the rocks become relatively gritty, and although they do not compare with the middle Wenlock beds in coarseness of grain they are not inappropriately called the Ludlow Grits. They consist of alternations of greywackes with mudstones and siltstones, the gritty rocks giving internal evidence of deposition by turbidity currents. They are coarsest in the Denbighshire Moors and in the Clwydian Range, there being few true grits interbedded with the finer rocks in the Llangollen area or in the Montgomeryshire outcrops. Cummins, on the multiple evidence of current direction, has inferred two major sources of sediment—a western landmass from which east-flowing currents carried the grits into Denbighshire, and a southern or south-western landmass from which north-flowing currents carried the mud and calcareous silts into Montgomeryshire.

Many of the sediments, particularly in the Ludlow Grits between Llansannan and Colwyn Bay, show intense disturbance of the bedding planes, which may be corrugated, minutely crumpled, and complexly folded on one another, and between which numerous slide-planes may be seen. Bands of such disturbed rock lie between unaltered ' normal ' mudstones in which the stratification shows no sign of deformation. The erosion of such rocks, especially where they are steeply dipping, produces a highly irregular topography. Boswell has attributed the structures in a number of instances to tectonic compression, disharmonic folding, and small-scale imbricate faulting; but O. T. Jones has put forward evidence leading to the conclusion that the disturbances were brought about by sliding and slumping of waterlogged muds at the time of deposition, and that the slumped beds moved southwards and south-eastwards down the flanks of an incipiently forming synclinal trough coincident with the main channel of turbidity current-flow inferred by Cummins.

The Ludlow beds, like the Wenlock, have been intensely folded and cleaved, and, especially in the Llangollen Syncline, have been worked for slates. Where the cleavage only affects the mudstones between the silty layers, the rocks may readily split along the bedding planes and have been worked for slabs.

No rocks of Upper Ludlow age have been found in place in North Wales, unless the Dinas Bran Beds near Llangollen, sandy shales and mudstones with a rich fauna of brachiopods, represent their earliest members. But the occurrence in the basal Carboniferous conglomerates of derived pebbles only slightly rounded containing Upper Ludlow fossils, including *Protochonetes striatellus*, both in the Llangollen district and on the northern flanks of the Denbighshire Moors near Abergele, leads to the conclusion (first drawn by Strahan and Walker) that the source of the pebbles is to be referred to rocks now concealed by the Carboniferous Limestone at no great distance from its marginal outcrop. Upper Ludlow beds were almost certainly deposited over much of north-eastern Wales, and their absence from the present surface is to be attributed largely to erosion before and during the time of deposition of the Limestone. In Clun Forest and the Kerry Hills south of Newtown, just beyond the limits of the North Wales area, there is an unbroken sequence from the Wenlock through the Ludlow and the Downton Series into the Old Red Sandstone.

VI. THE CALEDONIAN EARTH-MOVEMENTS

THE LONG PERIOD (spanning about 200 million years) of slow subsidence and deposition marked by the sediments of the Lower Palaeozoic geosyncline was followed by one of instability and intense earth-movement. The unconformities and contemporaneous oscillations of Lower Palaeozoic times, especially at the end of the Cambrian period, and again successively before the deposition of the Bala Series, of the Valentian Series, and of the Wenlock Series, were forerunners on a gentler scale of the grand folding and fracturing that occurred at the end of the Silurian period. At a few localities, as in the neighbouring district of the Welsh borderland, there was continuous deposition from Silurian into Old Red Sandstone times, but over the greater part of North Wales (as in other areas of north-western Europe) the rocks were thrown into folds that were in turn buckled into smaller and sharper structures. The least resistant rocks were squeezed, packed, and cleaved; while the more resistant were bent, broken, faulted, and overthrust, or caused to slide between the softer yielding masses, and to be piled up as mountain chains many thousands of feet above sea level. This major series of earth-movements is known as the Caledonian orogeny, a consequence of which was to impose upon North Wales (as upon other parts of Britain, notably the Lake District and Scotland) a general trend or strike of the axes of folding in a north-east to south-west direction: subsequent erosion has enhanced this effect by etching out the hard bands, so that the topographical ' grain ' of the country also follows the same broad alignment.

In North Wales, a controlling influence on this folding was exercised by the old worn-down Pre-Cambrian masses of Anglesey and the Bangor and Padarn ridges in the north-west, and the tougher members (the grits and conglomerates) of the Cambrian formation of the Harlech Dome on the west and south-west. These upfolded cores became resistant barriers which, though compelled under the intense compressive forces to yield to some extent, partly determined the structures induced in the softer sediments of the geosynclines. In places their effects were complemented by the relatively rigid masses of igneous rock inter-bedded with and intruded into the Ordovician sediments; and by similar (mainly doleritic) intrusions that were emplaced as an accompaniment of the main Caledonian movements. The final result was to produce two main synclinal tracts, complex in detail, with subsidiary minor folds: the Snowdon syncline to the north-west and the Central Wales syncline to the south-east of the Harlech–Derwen anticline, both of which trend in a general caledonoid (north-east to south-west) direction (see Fig. 30, p. 71).

As a major downfold the Snowdon syncline extends from the Llanrwst district through Snowdon and Moel Hebog, and then through the Lleyn peninsula to the sea at Porth Neigwl. It is a composite structure which in parts contains no dominant member, and of which the elements tend to display an arrangement in echelon and often to be out of alignment with the regional trend. The Central Wales syncline is also composite: it is well delineated by the narrow outcrop of Silurian rocks between Corwen and the ground about Lake Vyrnwy; but it pitches towards Central Wales where the Silurian outcrop expands into a series of minor folds between Machynlleth and Newtown.

The Harlech Dome (see Fig. 6, p. 17) is likewise not a simple structure. Its

principal component, the Dolwen pericline, strikes in a direction almost due
north-to-south: like the minor folds of the Snowdon syncline, it is thus not
aligned with the caledonoid trend of the main Harlech–Derwen anticline, and

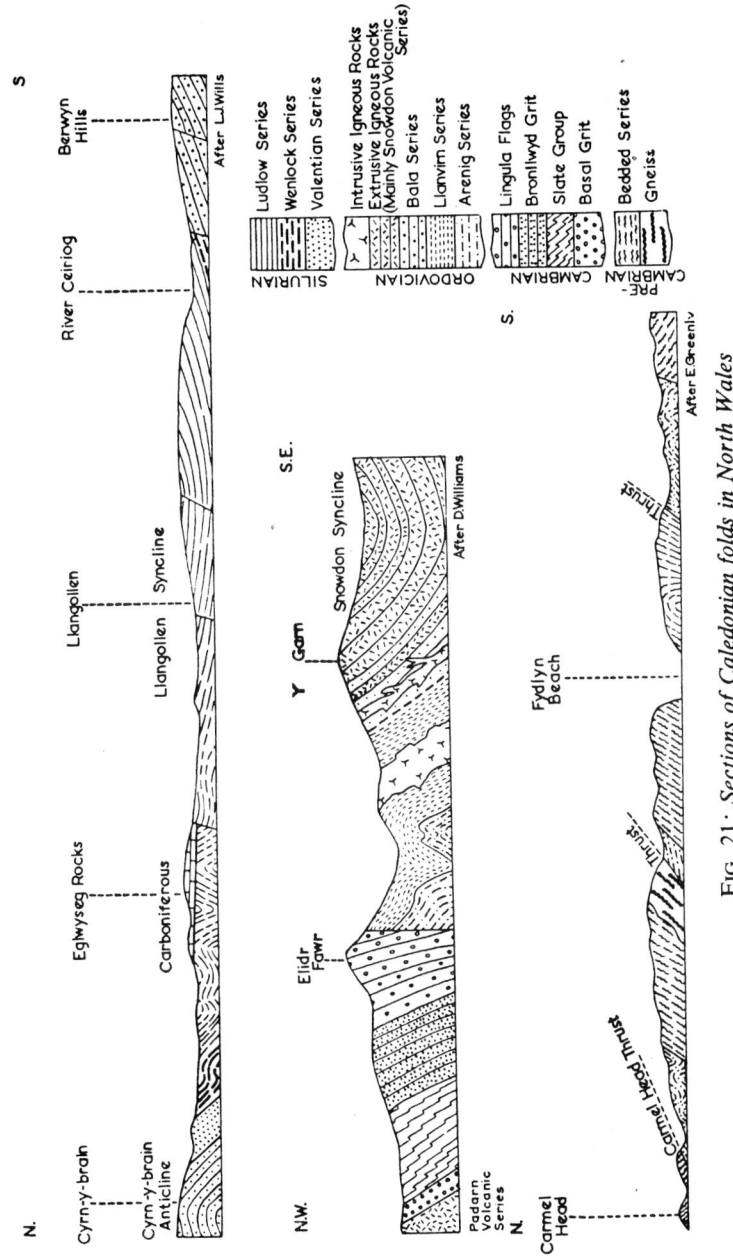

FIG. 21: *Sections of Caledonian folds in North Wales*

may owe its obliquity to a torque resulting from shear between the Cader Idris
range and the Snowdon syncline. The pericline is flanked by synclinal structures
to the west, which again show marked pitch and are in echelon. A minor

north-trending branch of the Dome carries a tongue of Upper Cambrian rocks into the Snowdon syncline between Portmadoc and Criccieth.

The Caledonian structures in the Lower Palaeozoic rocks of eastern North Wales are less closely packed. The decreasing influence and final burial of the pitching Harlech–Derwen anticline north-eastwards, combined with the shielding effects of the Longmynd barrier in Shropshire to the south-east, allowed a relative southward movement of the surface rocks to complement the northward underdrive of the deeper and more rigid western structures; and although there are caledonoid anticlinal tongues running south-westwards about Llanfyllin and Welshpool, the Ordovician rocks of the Berwyn anticline have a predominant east to west strike, which is paralleled by the axis of the Llangollen syncline to the north (a syncline that may be regarded as the bent and splaying analogue of the Central Wales syncline), and by the anticlines of Mynydd Cricor and Cyrn-y-brain. Within the major structures minor folds, usually in echelon, are again conspicuous.

The Snowdon syncline is often acutely folded in the Ordovician rocks (for instance about Snowdon itself and in the Dolwyddelan downfold); but in the Silurian tracts forming the greater part of the Denbighshire Moors Boswell has shown that, while in places the sediments may be closely plicated, the broad structure is that of an open shallow syncline in which the dominant strike is from east to west. Since the Carboniferous rocks of the western flank of the Vale of Clwyd rest unconformably on the truncated elements of the main structure, the Vale itself appears to be eroded in a post-Carboniferous downfold imposed upon a series of pre-Carboniferous plications. In similar paradox, the Silurian rocks of the post-Carboniferous horst of the Clwydian range possess an essentially synclinal structure (see Fig. 32, p. 75).

The Caledonian folds were accompanied by great faults, many of which behaved as fold-limb replacements. In Anglesey (Figs. 21, 22) and Lleyn, schists of the Mona Complex are thrust over Ordovician rocks; while the complexly resolved compressive forces between the Cambrian grits and the Ordovician

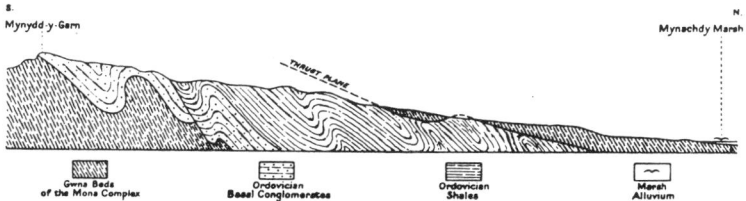

FIG. 22: *The Carmel Head thrust between Mynydd-y-Garn and Mynachdy Marsh*

Along the sole of the thrust (which locally is buckled) Pre-Cambrian Gwna Beds have moved southwards to over-ride Ordovician sediments. On the south side of the thrust, in the neighbourhood of Mynydd-y-Garn, the original sedimentary relations of the Ordovician rocks with the Pre-Cambrian are indicated by the thick basal Ordovician conglomerates, which contain abundant pebbles derived from the unconformably underlying Mona Complex.

grits and igneous rocks in the ground running from Portmadoc to Blaenau Ffestiniog sliced off whole tracts of country where slivers of rocks of very different ages are brought into contact in a zone of crushing that is in effect a huge fault-breccia. Farther south and east, the Ceunant–Gwernan faults near Dolgelley, the Bala–Talyllyn fault system, and the Bryneglwys fault (see Fig. 30, p. 71) show the effects of horizontal shear in more or less degree. At the same time there were initiated other faults, including the Llanelidan, Llangollen, and

Tanat Valley faults, which were to attain considerable importance at a later date under the renewed impetus of the late- or post-Carboniferous Hercynian stresses. On a smaller scale the fractures were comparatively minor in the deeper-seated rocks, but were very numerous, forming a grid system, in the Salopian mudstones and grits. The greater part of the Denbighshire Moors has been shown by Boswell to be a patterned mosaic of fault blocks superimposed on a large number of superficial ripples of low amplitude.

The igneous activity that either accompanied or closely followed the main movements is illustrated by a large intrusion of porphyrite occupying a volcanic vent near Llanyblodwel, south-west of Oswestry, and a sill of basic rock at Hendre, on the northern flank of the Berwyn Hills. Both these masses appear to have been injected later than the cleavage of the neighbouring sediments, but earlier than the deposition of the Carboniferous rocks. Fearnsides has similarly shown that on the northern flanks of the Harlech Dome intrusive activity took place after the initiation of cleavage; and in Anglesey many dykes and sills, running in a general caledonoid direction, were intruded at a late stage into the Lower Palaeozoic sediments, the majority consisting of dark basic dolerite, but a few, such as the felsite of Parys Mountain, being of intermediate or acid composition. Heated subterranean waters, possibly associated with these intrusions, introduced into the Ordovician and Silurian sediments sulphur compounds that crystallized out as the sulphides pyrites, blende, and galena. These, especially copper pyrites, are the chief ores that have been mined on Parys Mountain.

While the more rigid rock-types were being evenly folded and sharply faulted by the Caledonian movements, the softer shales and mudstones, and some of the finer-grained sandstones, flags, and ashes, were succumbing to the effects of pressure in a more intimate manner, and there was impressed upon them a secondary lamination, a slaty cleavage, not altogether different from the folia-tion observable in the Pre-Cambrian schists, that has enabled them to be split or cleaved into excellent roofing slates. The origin of the cleavage, so far as it is mechanically attributable to the effects of pressure, is partly due to a direct flattening of the particles contained in the rock, partly to a re-orientation of the particles so that they lie with their longer axes at right angles to the direction of pressure. Many of the minerals in the slaty rocks of North Wales have, how-ever, been regenerated by chemical changes from the original constituents under the conditions of dynamic metamorphism, so that as newly formed secondary minerals like sericitic mica and chlorite they grew with platy habit in directions normal to the direction of pressure: the parental rocks are then profoundly transformed, and their original nature may be more or less completely obliterated. The cleavage planes so produced are thus usually inclined at a high angle, and transgress the bedding or are parallel with the bedding according as the beds lie along the axes of folds or upon their flanks (see Fig. 9, p. 25). The trend of the planes of cleavage tends to be aligned with the axes of the major folds.

The development of slaty cleavage is obviously dependent upon the lithology of the parental rock and the intensity of lateral compression: it bears no relationship to the age of the rock. Thus the presence of suitable rocks in the sequence has resulted in the formation of excellent roofing slates in the Lower Cambrian rocks of the Bethesda–Nantlle belt, in the Upper Cambrian rocks of the Tremadoc area, in the Lower Ordovician of Blaenau Ffestiniog, in the Upper Ordovician of Corris and Aberllefenni, in the Valentian near Machynlleth, and in the Wenlock and Ludlow near Corwen and Llangollen.

VII. THE OLD RED SANDSTONE

THE CALEDONIAN earth-movements uplifted and crumpled the Lower Palaeozoic rocks to form a corrugated landmass of mountain ranges many thousands of feet in height. Only in south-eastern Montgomeryshire is there evidence of continuity of deposition from Silurian into Devonian times, though the Devonian rocks are of Old Red Sandstone facies bearing no signs of such normal open-sea environments as the underlying strata indicate. How far the Silurian–Devonian transition beds of the Downton Series persisted into the heart of North Wales is unknown; but they must have overlapped at comparatively short distance against a nearby coast, and the greater part of the north-western mountains were far above sea-level: in Anglesey the rock sequence provides clear evidence of the intensity of early Devonian erosion of the mountains in a deposit of Old Red Sandstone that rests with transgression variously on Ordovician and Pre-Cambrian rocks—before it was deposited Silurian and Ordovician sediments to a thickness of the order of perhaps 4,000 ft were removed from the neighbouring continental landmass.

The basal sediments of the Old Red Sandstone in Anglesey are conglomerates containing boulders, up to a foot in diameter, derived from local sources and transported no great distance before incorporation into the accumulating deposit. Source rocks can be identified in the Mona Complex (schist, gneiss, jasper, quartzite, and hornfels) and in the tougher Ordovician rocks (grit and hard mudstone); and transport was of such little range that dominant pebbles in any occurrence of conglomerates are commonly of the local basement rock. There follow in upward sequence more than 1,000 ft of fine-grained red and purple sandstones, marls, and cornstones, all of which give evidence of accumulation in restricted stretches of water under semi-arid conditions. Some of the deposits are loess-like, and may be the product of aeolian transport (though of aqueous deposition); and some give indication of deltaic running quicksands. The rocks have yielded no fossils, and their age is not surely known; but in general lithology they compare more nearly with the Lower than with the Upper Old Red Sandstone of the Welsh borderland and of South Wales.

Since the Old Red Sandstone is followed unconformably by strongly transgressive Carboniferous rocks, its absence from Anglesey (and from the north-western mainland) other than the narrow tongue running from the north-eastern coast southward to Llangefni (see Fig. 2, p. 7) is certainly in part due to overstep. Greenly has shown, however, that there is strong overlap within the Old Red Sandstone due to banking against a rising coast in the Llangefni neighbourhood; and the form of the present outcrops may be a vague and limited reflection of an elongate trench or gulf that ran deep into the contemporary mountains, a gulf to which the bulk of the formation was limited. Moreover, local overlap against cores of older rocks (Ordovician or Pre-Cambrian) suggests the existence of prominences or islands that were not submerged until a late stage of sedimentation, and provides a hint of contemporaneous geography.

VIII. THE CARBONIFEROUS SYSTEM

THE EROSIONAL EPISODE in North Wales initiated by the Caledonian earth-movements was not brought to a close until the Lower Carboniferous sea advanced over the area, beginning another cycle of deposition that ended with the Coal Measures. Even in Montgomeryshire, where thick Old Red Sandstone followed Silurian rocks conformably, there was renewed elevation and erosion in early Carboniferous times; and the small pocket of Old Red Sandstone in Anglesey is no more than an accidental residue preserved in an unusually deep trough that survived extinction after mid-Devonian warping. The Carboniferous rocks thus rest with great unconformity upon the Lower Palaeozoic rocks (Fig. 23), to which they offer a marked contrast in their relatively insignificant degree of folding and metamorphism.

The shallow shelf seas and deltas in which the Carboniferous rocks were deposited were markedly different from the 'oceanic' geosynclinal waters of Lower Palaeozoic times: in particular the conditions under which the grapto-litic shales, the greywackes, and the ribbon-banded mudstones and siltstones of the older systems were laid down appear to have had no representation, at any rate in the area that is now Britain, and nearly all the Carboniferous deposits accumulated at little distance from the neighbouring shores, and at depths rarely exceeding a few score of feet. Beginning with a series of clear-water off-shore limestones, they show in upward succession a progressive increase in the effects of a shallowing and a gradual silting-up of the sea in which they were deposited, until the sediments of later Carboniferous times are characteristically of delta and swamp facies. The Carboniferous system can consequently be divided into three broad groups of strata, indicating these changing conditions—groups, however, between which the lines of demarcation are not abrupt and are arbitrarily defined. The three divisions are:

3. COAL MEASURES: comprising sediments deposited when the sea had become silted up. They are therefore almost entirely of terrigenous origin, and accumulated in swamps and marshes drained by streams of fresh or brackish water. They contain only thin and rare layers of truly marine origin. The fossils are chiefly plants and freshwater 'mussels'.
2. MILLSTONE GRIT: also largely of terrigenous origin (sands, silts, clays and muds) but most of it formed under marine delta conditions, and containing shales and impure limestones with a marine fauna mainly of molluscs (goniatites and lamellibranchs) and brachiopods.
1. CARBONIFEROUS or MOUNTAIN LIMESTONE: comprising a thick series of relatively pure limestones formed in water to which, although shallow, very little material from the neighbouring land was being transported; and usually containing abundantly many kinds of invertebrate fossils.

CARBONIFEROUS LIMESTONE

The transgressive Carboniferous sea, like an incoming tide, at first covered only the lowland tracts of the peneplain carved in later Old Red Sandstone times. The first of its deposits, the terrigenous Basement Beds of the Car-boniferous Limestone Series, thus occur only restrictedly, as, for example, in the Llangollen Syncline between the uplifted hills of the Berwyns and Cyrn-y-brain. By the end of Lower Carboniferous times the greater part of North

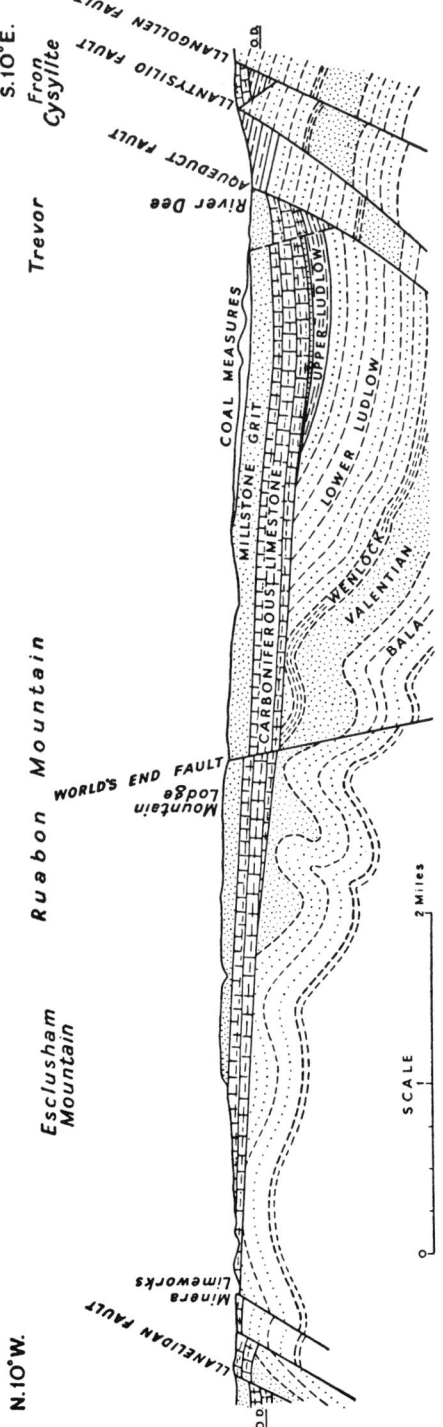

FIG. 23: *Overstep of the Carboniferous rocks across the folded Lower Palaeozoic rocks, and overlap within the Lower Carboniferous rocks, Ruabon Mountain*

The section, drawn across the Cyrn-y-Brain anticline and the Llangollen syncline, also shows the different degrees of deformation of the Lower Palaeozoic rocks and the Carboniferous.

(A.3136)

A. Eglwyseg Rocks, Llangollen

Plate VIII

B. Yr Eifl projecting above the coastal plain of Ordovician sediments

(A.6502)

Wales, except perhaps the cores of the western mountains, was submerged beneath the sea and was buried under calcareous deposits that in places attain a thickness of nearly 3,000 ft; the skeletal remains of corals, brachiopods, and crinoids materially contributed to these deposits.

The subsidence of the land and the return of the sea after the continental conditions of the Old Red Sandstone did not take place, however, until much of Carboniferous time had elapsed; and while the major part of the Mountain Limestone of South Wales, the Mendips, and the North of England was being deposited, North Wales still remained an area of barren hills and storm-swept plains. Thus, despite its great thickness, the Limestone of the area is wholly or mainly equivalent only to the uppermost division, the *Dibunophyllum* Zone, of other districts. This is proved by the abundant corals and brachiopods that are found in it (Fig. 24): of the corals *Dibunophyllum* itself, various species of *Lithostrotion* (including *L. portlocki*, *L. junceum*, and *L. martini*), and *Lonsdaleia* are important; and of the brachiopods, species of *Spirifer*, *Chonetes*, and *Productus*, and the characteristic *Daviesiella comoides* and *D. llangollensis*.

To the east of the fragmented outcrops of Anglesey and the neighbouring mainland, the Lower Carboniferous rocks are seen in two main sub-parallel arcs. One runs more or less south-eastwards and southwards from the Great Orme along the western flank of the Vale of Clwyd to Llanelidan. The other runs along the eastern flank of the Clwydian Range from Prestatyn by Halkyn Mountain to Llandegla; it is stepped eastwards to Minera by the Llanelidan fault, and then passes southwards by Llangollen (Pl. VIIIA) to Llanymynech,

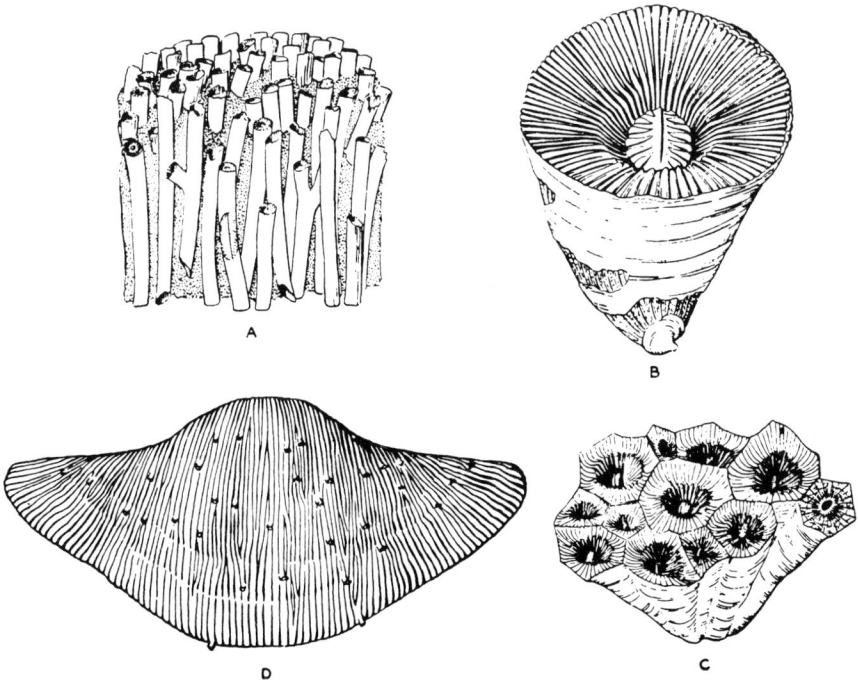

FIG. 24: *Carboniferous Limestone fossils* (All natural size).

A, *Lithostrotion junceum* (Fleming); **B,** *Dibunophyllum bipartitum* (M'Coy); **C,** *Lonsdaleia floriformis* (Martin) forma *crassiconus* (M'Coy); **D,** *Productus (Gigantoproductus) latissimus* J. Sowerby.

transgressing unconformably the strike of the Lower Palaeozoic rocks of the Llangollen syncline and the Berwyn anticline almost at right angles. Small faulted outcrops occur on the eastern side of the Vale of Clwyd against the great Vale of Clwyd fault, but their structural relations with the main areas are difficult to determine. In a crude and general sense the peripheral alignment of the Carboniferous outcrops about the Lower Palaeozoic hinterland is a reflection of a physique that controlled Carboniferous sedimentation and that is an inheritance both of Carboniferous drowning and Hercynian doming.

Along the eastern outcrops flanking the Vale of Clwyd, the Llangollen syncline, and the Berwyn anticline, the normal calcareous deposits of the Carboniferous Limestone are underlain along part of their outcrop by a series of near-shore deposits, consisting of conglomerates, sandstones, and shales, with occasional fine-grained limestones. These rocks, the Basement Beds, are often purple, red, or mottled green and red in colour, and look not unlike beds of Old Red Sandstone, to which they were referred by the older geologists. In places, however, they contain a typically marine brachiopod fauna, showing them to have been formed in the Carboniferous sea, and their ' continental ' appearance is probably to be attributed to their being the first ' washings ' from the old deeply-eroded land surface of post-Silurian days. It is not improbable also that in part they were deposited in very shallow-water ' lagoons ' which were favourable to the oxidation of the iron compounds. Being the littoral deposits of a transgressive sea, they are not everywhere of the same age. They give place upwards to normal limestones, in which the changing conditions of deposition are reflected in slight differences in lithology and fossil content: the work of Hind, Stobbs, and especially G. H. Morton, has shown that the main mass can be divided into the following broad groups of strata:

(iv) **Black Limestone of north Flintshire.** A fine-grained muddy limestone deposited not far from a neighbouring shore, and containing, besides the usual marine fauna of corals and brachiopods, well-preserved drifted plant remains. In south Flintshire and Denbighshire the Black Limestone appears to pass laterally into a series of sandstones, sandy limestones, and dark bituminous shales (the Sandy Limestone Group). Maximum thickness about 500 ft.

(iii) **Upper Grey Limestone.** Fossiliferous crinoidal limestones. The uppermost beds contain quartz grains and pebbles, and are transitional in places into the overlying Sandy Limestone Group. Maximum thickness about 800 ft.

(ii) **Middle White Limestone.** Essentially similar to the Upper Grey Limestone, but containing a slightly less proportion of non-calcareous matter. Maximum thickness about 1,500 ft.

(i) **Lower Grey and Brown Limestone.** Limestone containing a greater or less proportion of muddy and sandy sediment. Plant remains occur in places, drifted from nearby land. Some of the beds are pseudobreccias, and calcite mudstones are common in the lower part. Maximum thickness about 950 ft.

[Basement Beds. Very impure calcite mudstones, calcareous sandstones, shales, and conglomerates. Maximum thickness about 300 ft.]

In places the Lower Brown Limestone, as near the axis of the Cyrn-y-brain anticline, or the Lower Brown and Middle White limestones together, as near the axis of the Berwyn anticline, may be absent. Although the evidence is not everywhere conclusive, it seems clear that as the Lower Palaeozoic rocks of the core of the Caledonian mountain mass ('St. George's Land') were gradually overstepped by the Carboniferous Limestone, successively higher beds within the Limestone, overlapping those below to cover greater and greater areas, were banked against hills and headlands that remained emergent until a relatively late date. The coincidence of such eminences with anticlinal cores in the Lower Palaeozoic rocks may be a sign of continued, if gentle, arching during Carboniferous sedimentation (see Fig. 25).

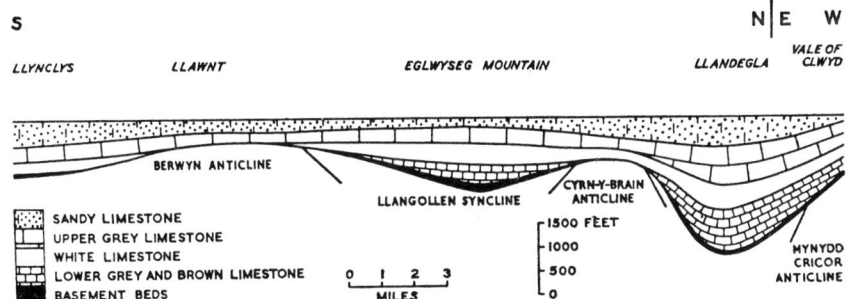

FIG. 25: *Lateral changes in the Carboniferous Limestone Series on the flanks of the Berwyn anticline and the Llangollen syncline*

Traced northwards, from Denbighshire into Flintshire, the sandy limestones at the top of the Limestone Series appear to pass laterally into the Black Limestone, presumably at increased distance from the source of coarse detritus. Banded cherts with thin intervening shales follow immediately upon the Black Limestone and may also be of Lower Carboniferous age: Sargent has considered them to be of contemporaneous origin, and to have been deposited in a more or less land-locked shallow lagunary basin.

Along the eastern flanks of the Clwydian Range (Fig. 26) the Carboniferous Limestone reaches its maximum development in North Wales, where nearly 3,000 ft of rock, almost all of it richly fossiliferous limestone, is nevertheless the representative of only the upper members of the group of other areas in Britain. In the northernmost outcrops, around Newmarket and Prestatyn, the sequence is appreciably thinner, and the main mass of limestones is purer so that the three broad lithological groups are not readily distinguished. There are also developed patch reefs, described by Neaverson, containing abundant brachiopods in a fine-grained calcite-mudstone matrix, that, like the similar reefs in Derbyshire and Yorkshire, project nowadays as prominent knolls above the flanking evenly stratified limestone beds. The Black Limestone of Teilia, near Prestatyn, is exceptionally rich in well preserved plant remains.

The narrow outcrops of Carboniferous Limestone on the western flanks of the Vale of Clwyd are not well known, partly because of the faulting that occurred towards the end of Carboniferous times. Neaverson has shown most of the rocks to belong to the lower part of the *Dibunophyllum* Zone. Many of the limestones are dark and sandy, and were deposited at no great distance from the contemporary coast. They are progressively overlapped in the outcrops about Cyrn-y-brain; and the coral-bearing limestones of the small remote outlier of Hafod-y-Calch near Corwen, which must have been near the limits of Lower Carboniferous sedimentation, lie high in the *Dibunophyllum* Zone.

The sequence in the northernmost mainland exposures of the Great Orme and the ground east of Conway, described in detail by Smyth and Neaverson, is not greatly dissimilar from that of the main outcrop to the east; it is peculiar, however, in containing a thick series of dolomitic beds at its base.

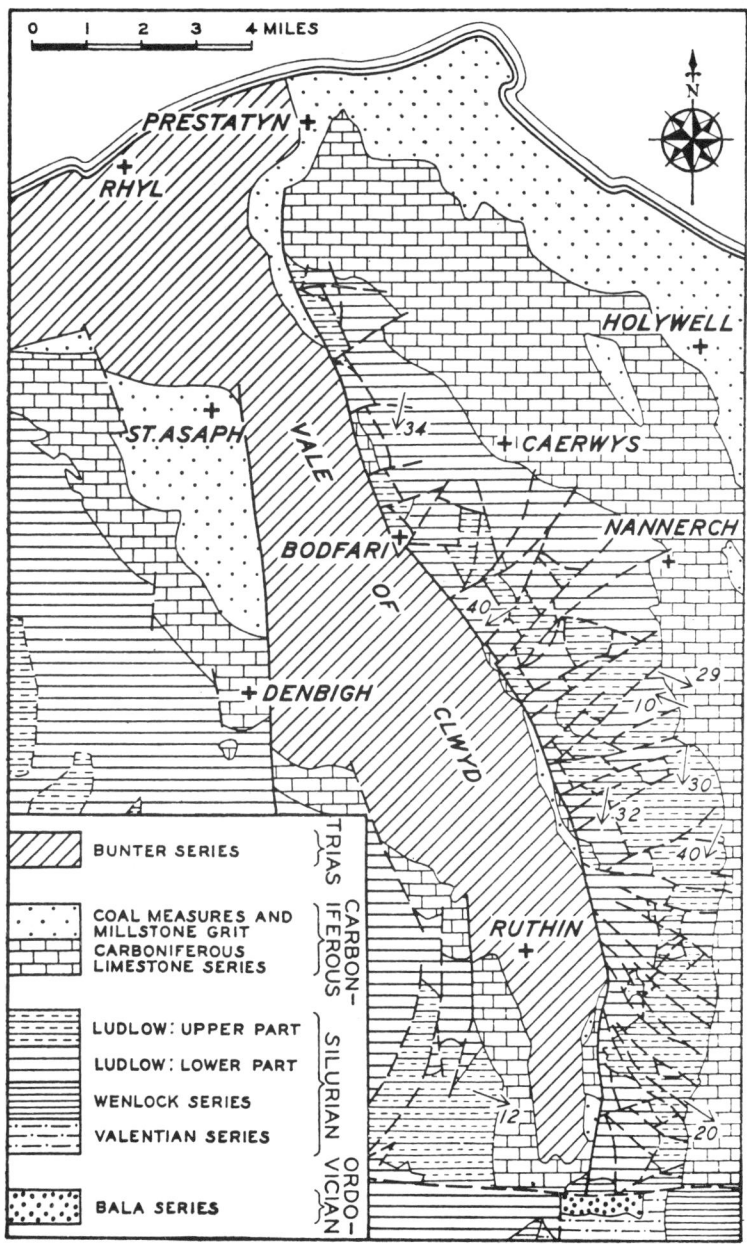

Fig. 26: *Geological map of the Vale of Clwyd and the Clwydian Range*

Still farther to the west, in Anglesey, the Carboniferous Limestone rests unconformably upon the Old Red Sandstone, which it oversteps to rest upon Lower Palaeozoic rocks and upon rocks of the Mona Complex. Greenly has demonstrated that, as on the mainland of North Wales, the strata are confined wholly or almost wholly to the *Dibunophyllum* Zone, and the unconformity separating the Limestone from the Old Red Sandstone is of the same order of magnitude as the unconformity on the mainland. The basal beds of the Limestone are not everywhere of the same age, or of the same lithological nature. They are conglomeratic and sandy where the succession is thickly developed (when they constitute the Lligwy Sandstone), but higher beds of the Limestone may be seen in places visibly to overlap the lower against contemporary headlands and islands (much in the same way as the upper beds overlap the lower against the hills flanking the Llangollen depression), so that the basal Lligwy Sandstone constitutes a transgressive facies and mounts to higher and higher geological horizons as it is traced south-westwards. This overlap is an indication of the gradual deepening of the Lower Carboniferous sea, and consequently of decrease in the size of the land area from which the sandy material was obtained: where maximum overlap occurs, therefore, the basal beds are much less arenaceous than in areas where the succession is more complete. Above the sandy beds there occur nearly 1,000 ft of fossiliferous limestones with subsidiary shales and sandstones, like the limestones of the mainland farther east; they are capped, as in Flintshire, by a thickness of bedded cherts with thin limestones. A comparable succession is seen on the neighbouring mainland of Arvon. It is possible that the whole of the Carboniferous Limestone was overlapped in the extreme south-west of the island: the Menai region was then a deep gulf or embayment separating the contemporary hills of Anglesey from the main mass of 'St. George's Land' to the south.

MILLSTONE GRIT

The only extensive outcrops of Millstone Grit in North Wales are found in Flintshire and Denbighshire, where the series occupies a tract to the east of the Carboniferous Limestone, running from Prestatyn southwards by Flint and Mold to Ruabon Mountain and Oswestry. In this distance of over thirty miles it shows marked changes in lithology: the northern sequence is one mainly of shale (the Holywell Shales), the southern mainly of sandstone (the Cefn-y-fedw Sandstone). Formerly this facies distinction caused difficulties in correlation, the Holywell Shales being regarded in part as belonging to the Coal Measures, the Cefn-y-fedw Sandstone in part as belonging to the Carboniferous Limestone Series. But work by Lloyd and Jones, and particularly by Wood, has now proved them to be almost precisely contemporaneous.

The Holywell Shales consist of some 400 to 600 ft of blue and black carbonaceous shales with cementstones and some thin coaly layers. Interbedded are ribs or thicker seams of sandstone, grit, quartzite, and ganister. Some of the shale bands are highly siliceous and pass into pure cherts. Fossils indicate the presence of most of the goniatite zones of the Millstone Grit (Fig. 27): the *Eumorphoceras* Zone contains *Eumorphoceras bisulcatum*, *Cravenoceras*, and *Anthracoceras paucilobum;* the *Homoceras* Zone, *Homoceratoides prereticulatus* *Homoceras eostriolatum*, *Anthracoceras*, and *Dimorphoceras;* the *Reticuloceras* Zone, the most widely exposed member, *Reticuloceras inconstans*, *Reticuloceras reticulatum*, *Reticuloceras bilingue*, and *Homoceras striolatum;* the *Gastrioceras*

Zone, *Gastrioceras cancellatum*, *Gastrioceras crenulatum*, and *Reticuloceras superbilingue*. The Holywell Shales of the Flint area are succeeded by a well-bedded fine-grained sandstone, the Gwespyr Sandstone, 300 ft thick: underlain by beds with *Gastrioceras cumbriense* and immediately overlain by Coal Measures, it may be regarded as the topmost member of the Millstone Grit.

The Cefn-y-fedw Sandstone, reaching perhaps a maximum thickness of 600 ft in Ruabon Mountain, is dominantly a series of grits, conglomerates, sandstones, and quartzites, originally more or less calcareous but now decalcified. At the same time it contains considerable thicknesses of interbedded shale

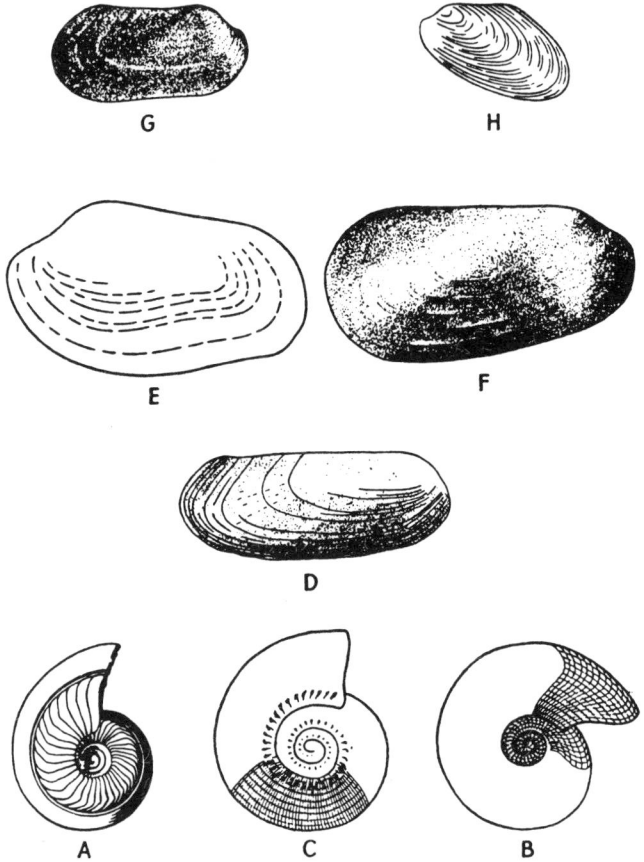

Fig. 27: *Upper Carboniferous fossils* (All natural size).

A, *Eumorphoceras bisulcatum* Girty; **B,** *Reticuloceras reticulatum* (Phillips); **C,** *Gastrioceras cancellatum* Bisat; **D,** *Anthraconaia lenisulcata* (Trueman); **E,** *Carbonicola communis* Davies and Trueman; **F,** *A. modiolaris* (J. de C. Sowerby); **G,** *A. pulchra* (Hind); **H,** *Anthraconauta phillipsii* (Williamson).

and shaly cherts which in places have yielded goniatites permitting correlation with the Holywell Shales to the north. As the group is followed southwards into the Oswestry district there is both a reduction in thickness (to about 280 ft) and an increase in the proportion of arenaceous material, with shale insignificantly represented. The initially calcareous nature of much of the Cefn-y-fedw Sandstone is reflected in the relatively great abundance and variety of fossils it contains. Goniatites and such lamellibranchs as *Posidonia, Posidoniella*, and *Dunbarella* are almost exclusively confined to the shaly layers; but in the more massive beds are found numbers of brachiopods, including species of *Spirifer, Athyris (Cleiothyridina), Productus, Chonetes, Schizophoria*, and Orthotetids, forming a faunal assemblage like that of the underlying Carboniferous Limestone. In Denbighshire the topmost bed of the Cefn-y-fedw Sandstone is the conglomeratic and felspathic Aqueduct Grit, the approximate time-equivalent of the Gwespyr Sandstone.

In the neighbourhood of Prestatyn Neaverson has noted the occurrence of a remanié bed at the base of the Millstone Grit resting on a pitted surface of the Carboniferous Limestone, which may indicate an erosional break between the two series.

Small exposures of what formerly was regarded as Millstone Grit occur in Anglesey, where coarse, rusty, gritty sandstones with subordinate interbedded shales are found mainly about Bodorgan. Fossils from shales near the middle of the group include *Gastrioceras listeri*, however, a typical fossil of one of the lowest zones of the Coal Measures; and it is probable that no true Millstone Grit is preserved. The sandstones rest transgressively on older rocks; the underlying surface of the Carboniferous Limestone is commonly weathered and potholed; and when that formation is completely overstepped along the flanks of the Malldraeth basin and the sandstones rest on Pre-Cambrian rocks of the Mona Complex, they sometimes (as near Bodorgan) are seen to be banked against a contemporaneous cliffed shore-line of schists.

COAL MEASURES

An increasing proportion of terrigenous material and a declining influence of open-sea neritic marine conditions are features characterizing the uppermost beds of the Carboniferous Limestone, and in intensified degree they enable the Millstone Grit conveniently to be distinguished on a lithological basis from the older formation. In the succeeding Coal Measures the areas of marine flats and deltas gradually silted up, and the British environment became one of brackish and freshwater swamps in and along the borders of which the plants that periodically formed the coal seams flourished. In North Wales the local land area at this time appears to have been the residual mountains of 'St. George's Land'—mountains which had been reduced to a peneplain by continued erosion since the Caledonian uplift, and which were drained by rivers, at times fast-flowing, that carried detritus into a basin of sedimentation that lay to the north and east.

At the present day the largest outcrop of Coal Measures in the region extends from the Point of Air at the mouth of the Dee Estuary southwards to the neighbourhood of Oswestry. The easterly regional dip causes the Carboniferous strata to plunge beneath the younger New Red Sandstone of the Cheshire plain (Fig. 28); and it is probable that in this synclinal tract the Coal Measures of North Wales unite with those of the Lancashire and Staffordshire coalfields. In places boreholes have proved their occurrence at depth; and vast amounts of unworked coal possibly lie buried in easternmost Denbighshire and Flintshire, though whether it lies near enough to the surface to be profitably exploited is not yet known.

Farther west, outcrops of Upper Carboniferous rocks flanking the Trias suggest that in the lower reaches of the Vale of Clwyd a small buried coalfield

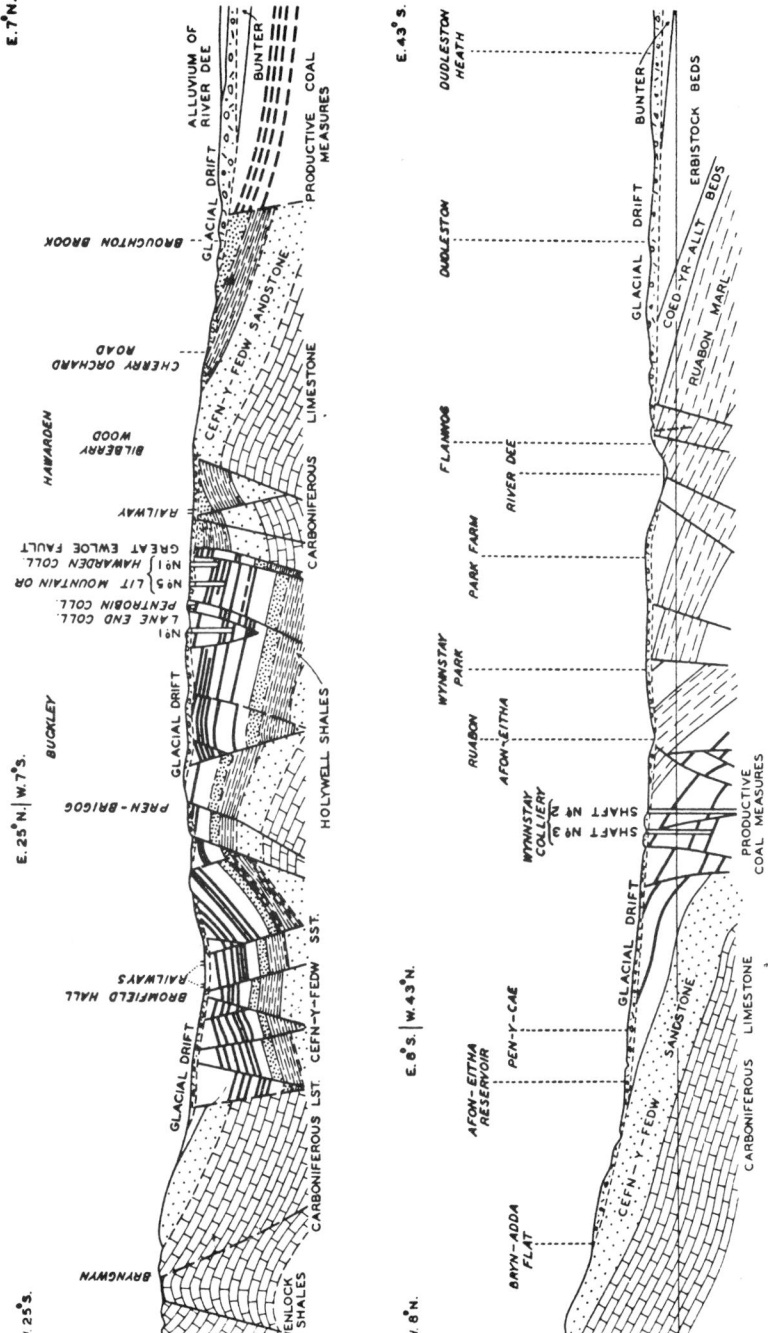

FIG. 28: *Comparative sections across the Flintshire and Denbighshire coalfields*

The sections are taken from the New Series 1-inch Geological Survey Maps Nos. 108 and 121.

may have workable coals at no great depth. In Anglesey a number of pits have been sunk in the past into the Coal Measures of the comparable Malldraeth syncline.

The changing environments of deposition during Upper Carboniferous times are reflected in the lithological succession of the Coal Measures. The earlier sediments appear to have accumulated under warm humid conditions, with growths of luxuriant vegetation providing an abundance of fossils: the strata then consist mainly of dark blue and grey pyritous shales and clay, with abundant coal seams, forming the Productive Measures. The later sediments, on the other hand, suggest the onset of truly ' continental ' conditions inimical to plant growth: as the Upper Coal Series they contain no workable coal seams.

During the accumulation of these non-marine shallow-water deposits, slight earth-movements, occurring along lines of warping instituted in pre-Carboniferous times, were again in evidence. And while in the sinking (synclinal) basins the whole sequence of the Coal Measures is present and thickly developed, along the intervening stationary or rising (anticlinal) tracts the measures were thinned off or actually denuded, with the development of local unconformities. Contemporaneous erosion is especially manifest at the base of the barren Upper Coal Measures where they straddle the crests of the folds. One of the more important of these contemporary upwarps became prominent towards the close of Productive Coal Measures times, and tended to separate the Flintshire and Denbighshire coal basins. Thus while many of the beds of the Productive Measures, including the principal coal seams, are traceable over most of the area, the Upper Measures are notably different in the two counties (Fig. 29). As a whole, deposition seems to have been nearer sea-level in Flintshire, where loss of coal in ' washouts ' is less common and less extensive than in Denbighshire.

In Flintshire the Productive Measures total nearly 2,000 ft at their maximum, and include some eighteen workable seams of coal, varying in thickness from 1 ft to $13\frac{1}{2}$ ft. Of these the principal are the Main Coal, the Wall-and-Bench Coal, and the Yard Coal which passes laterally into the well-known Cannel Coal of Leeswood. All these coals are traceable with little change in character throughout the coalfields of North Wales. Most of them are steam-raising coals of different qualities. Sporadically throughout the succession of shales and clays with coal seams there occur beds of coarse sandstone that do not persist over such large areas as the finer-grained and carbonaceous deposits; of these, the Hollin Rock is perhaps the chief. Thin beds of ironstone are also of not uncommon occurrence.

In Denbighshire the Productive Measures are, as in Flintshire, mainly characterized by a general predominance of clays and shales, but they contain a larger proportion of sandy shales and sandstones than is found to the north, the principal sandy bed being the Cefn Rock (which lies at a higher horizon than the Hollin Rock).

In the synclinal basins of Flintshire. the highest coal-bearing grey shales are succeeded by a group of rocks, unlike any of the underlying beds of the Productive Coal Measures, consisting of hard fine-grained quartzose and softer felspathic sandstones. In colour the sandstones are white, grey, or greenish, but superficially they are stained purple, crimson or yellow. They tend to grade into fine siliceous ' clunch ', of which one bed passes into purple, black, and grey marl: this is the Buckley Fireclay, used for the manufacture of fire- and acid-resisting bricks and tiles. Similar fireclays underlying some of the coals, and a few beds of fine-grained quartzite (ganister), are also worked elsewhere, though not to such an extent, for the manufacture of bricks.

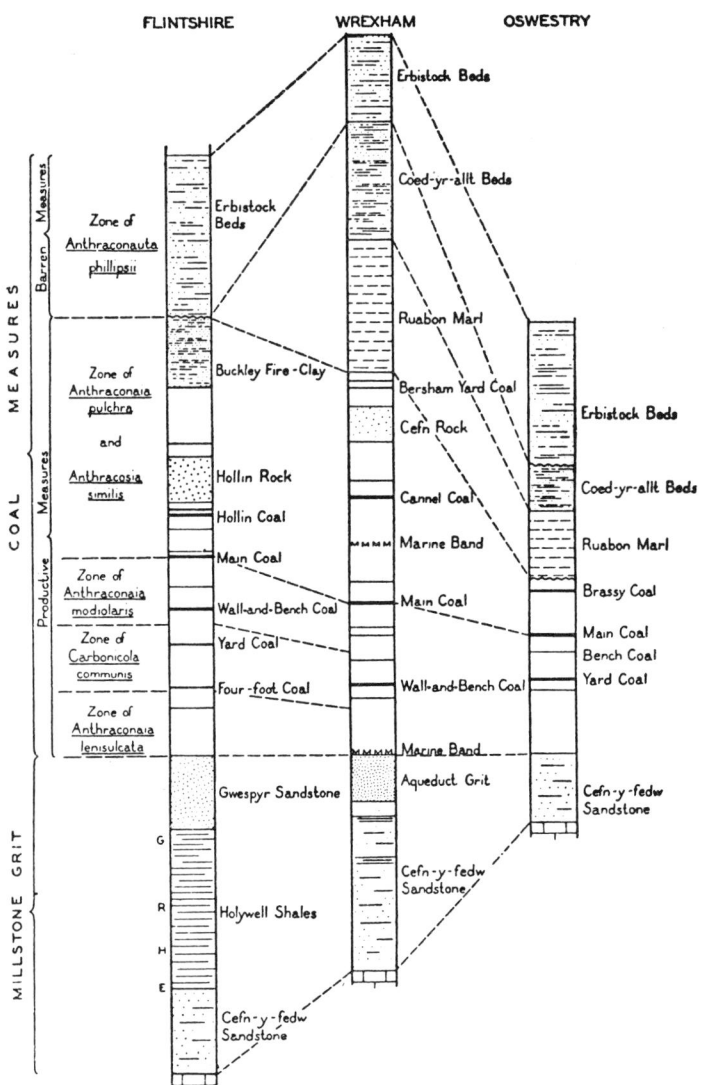

FIG. 29: *Vertical sections in the Upper Carboniferous rocks of Flintshire and Denbighshire*

Plants are abundant at certain horizons in the Productive Measures, but 'mussels' and other animals are comparatively rare. The work of Wood, however, has shown that, marked by their index fossils, the zones of *Anthraconaia lenisulcata* (with *Anthraconaia bellula*), *Carbonicola communis* (with *C. rhomboidalis*, *Anthracosia aquilina*, and *Naiadites triangularis*), *Anthraconaia modiolaris* (with *Carbonicola oslancis*, *Anthracosia aquilina*, *Anthracosia phrygiana*, and *Naiadites*), and *Anthraconaia pulchra* and *Anthracosia similis* (with *Anthracosia nitida*, *A. acutella*, *and A. atra*) occur in Flintshire and northern Denbighshire (Fig. 27). Marine beds are known from three horizons: immediately above the Aqueduct Grit at Trevor, *Gastrioceras subcrenatum,*

Dunbarella [*Pterinopecten*] *papyracea*, and *Posidoniella multirugata* are characteristic of the lowest horizon in the Coal Measures; a band with brachiopods above the Four-foot seam may be the equivalent of the Wernffrwd marine band of South Wales; and a band in the *similis–pulchra* Zone is probably the equivalent of the Cefn Coed marine band of South Wales and the Dukinfield of Lancashire. A persistent fish-bed forms the roof of the Wall-and-Bench Coal throughout its extent in Flintshire and the northern part of Denbighshire.

The Upper Coal Measures differ from the Productive Measures, not only in being without workable coal seams, but also in the nature of the shales and sandstones. These tend to be predominantly red in colour, partly because of a changing environment from stagnant swamps with abundant decaying humus to faster-moving waters in which peats could not accumulate or much plant debris remain to reduce the iron compounds from a rusty ferric to a grey-blue ferrous state. There can be little question, however, that the red beds also indicate an increasing aridity of climate towards the end of Upper Carboniferous times, and were a prelude to the desert deposits of the New Red Sandstone. Formerly some of the members were classed as Permian and only the occasional occurrence of typical Carboniferous fossils in them is now convincing proof that they belong to the older system.

The Upper Coal Measures are traceable from near Flint in the Dee estuary southwards to Oswestry. They are most typically represented in the Denbighshire and west Shropshire part of the coalfield, where the succession is as follows:

(iii) Erbistock Beds: purple and red variegated sandstones, with some marls, conglomerates and breccias. There are a few thin unworkable coals, together with fine-grained muddy *Spirorbis* limestones. About 3,000 ft thick.

(ii) Coed-yr-allt-Beds: greenish-white calcareous sandstones with marl bands and *Spirorbis* and ostracod limestones. About 520 ft thick.

(i) Ruabon Marl: purple, red, and green mottled marls, similar to the red marls of the Trias and much used in brick and tile manufacture. Thin *Spirorbis* limestones, with fish remains, occur near the top, while coarser pebbly grits (Espley rocks) occur sporadically in the lower part. About 1,100 ft thick.

Nearly all the recorded fossils have been found towards the top of the Ruabon Marl, the chief kinds being molluscs (*Anthraconauta phillipsii* and *Anthraconauta calcifera*), fishes (*Gyracanthus*, *Megalichthys*), annelids (*Spirorbis*), ostracods (*Carbonita*), and a few plants. The molluscs show the beds to be contemporaneous with part of the Upper Coal Measures of South Wales, Staffordshire, and other coalfields.

The intra-Carboniferous movements that caused slight flexuring during the deposition of the Productive Coal Measures became more intense before deposition of the Upper Measures, and, although never so great as to be appreciable in any one exposure, they were of sufficient magnitude to give rise to mild doming on the Flintshire area. Thus, while deposition was practically continuous in north Denbighshire, the upper part of the Productive Measures suffered erosion in Flintshire, the successive beds of the Upper group showing progressive overlap on to the dome as they are traced northwards. Over the greater part of the Flintshire Coalfield, therefore, only the Erbistock Beds of the Upper Measures are present, resting unconformably upon eroded Productive Measures.

In the southern part of the basin in the neighbourhood of Oswestry, on the other hand, slight elevation occurred after the deposition of the Coed-yr-allt Beds; and towards the south the Erbistock Beds gradually transgress to rest on lower and lower horizons of the Ruabon Marl. At the same time the Ruabon Marl is itself transgressive across the Productive Measures and comes to rest on a low horizon in the *similis–pulchra* Zone (see Fig. 29.).

The Coal Measures in Anglesey display a comparable succession of Red Measures, 700 ft thick, overlying some 1,000 ft of Productive Measures. The Productive Measures, however, although they have been mined for coal, do not crop out at the surface, as they are covered by a considerable thickness of alluvium and Glacial drift under and along the borders of Malldraeth Marsh. Their fossils contain molluscs (*Carbonicola*), a number of fishes, and many plants.

IX. THE HERCYNIAN EARTH-MOVEMENTS AND MINERALIZATION

THE REPEATED intra-Carboniferous oscillations, non-sequences, and unconformities were but the preliminaries to a great earth storm second in magnitude
only to the Caledonian orogeny. In Britain deformation reached its greatest
intensity in the south, particularly in South Wales and in Devon and Cornwall.
On the Continent it is well seen in the Harz Mountains, whence it derives its
name of ' Hercynian '. The drive in Britain was from the south, and the earth-
ripples broke against a broad belt of old rocks, Lower Palaeozoic and Pre-
Cambrian in age, that had been packed and hardened by the earlier Caledonian
movements. North Wales was therefore relatively protected from the most
intense disturbances, and the movements engendered comparatively gentle
folds, with little crumpling and thrusting and no cleavage. There was, however,
much fracturing including an accentuation of faults that had been in existence
since Lower Palaeozoic times, and the establishment of faults along new lines
that were influenced by the trends of the earlier structures. (See Fig. 30)

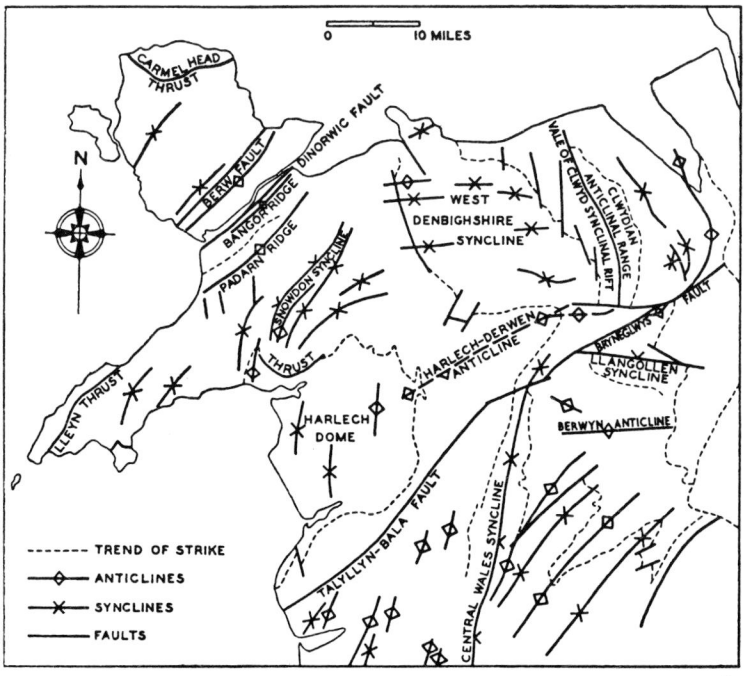

FIG. 30: *Sketch-map showing the distribution of the major structures of
North Wales*

Although the impulse was from a southerly direction, resistance afforded by
the older rocks to its direct forward drive seems to have been great, and the
energy of movement was diverted to a considerable degree along subtangential
components following old Caledonoid lines of weakness. Thus movement

71

appears to have been primarily lateral along the Bala, Bryn Eglwys, Llanelidan, and Llangollen faults, the horizontal displacement of the rocks on the south side being eastwards or north-eastwards relative to the rocks on the north side. Thus the Carboniferous Limestone outcrop running from the coast to Llandegla was displaced some four miles eastwards to Minera; and again some four miles eastwards along the Aqueduct fault farther south (Fig. 31); and the comparable sinistral displacement of about two miles proved by Jehu along the Bala–Talyllyn fault in the Lower Palaeozoic rocks near Towyn may also have a large Hercynian component. Such tear faults commonly show great variations in amount and direction of apparent throw.

Anticlinal axes transverse to and curving round the nose of the Harlech–Derwen anticline were accentuated. Examples are provided by the Clwydian Range of Silurian rocks (the *inner crescentic anticline* of C. B. Wedd), of which the uplift was accompanied by the great Vale of Clwyd Fault (see Figs. 26, 32), and by the complementary synclinal rift of the Vale of Clwyd; and by the so-called Horse-shoe anticline (the *outer crescentic anticline*), trending from Mynydd Cricor through Cyrn-y-brain eastwards and northwards through the Flintshire coalfield to the Dee estuary. The northern half of an ideally symmetrical Mynydd Cricor dome was not developed when the country south of the Llanelidan Fault was driven during its eastward movement against the northern fault block. The sector between the Llanelidan and Bryn Eglwys faults and the still larger sector between the Bryn Eglwys and Llangollen faults, were rotated clockwise with the production of the great curving Minera faults. Farther south the Berwyn Hills themselves north of the Tanat Fault also participated in similar torsional movements (Figs. 30, 31). Comparable structures have been recognized by Boswell in the Silurian rocks of the Denbighshire moors.

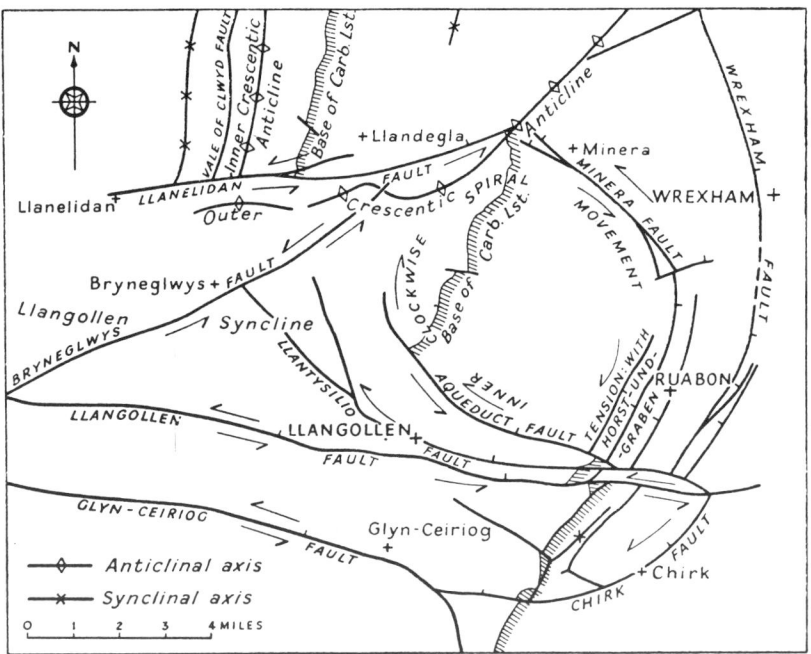

FIG. 31: *Map to illustrate Hercynian folding, faulting and torsional strain in the Llangollen area, North Wales*

Accompanying these major fractures there were also produced in areas of tension many smaller faults, very clearly displayed along the Carboniferous Limestone outcrop from the sea to Minera. Some of these faults, particularly in the coalfields, gave rise to typical horst and graben structure—small uplifted fault-blocks separated by downthrown segments.

In Anglesey the Hercynian structures were controlled by the earlier Caledonian, and have a general north-east to south-west trend. Two principal downfolds may be recognised, in both of which Upper Carboniferous rocks are preserved: one forms the floor of the Malldraeth depression; the other in part underlies the Menai Straits, and flanks the Ordovician rocks of the Arvonian mainland. They were accompanied in their formation by major strike faulting, the Berw fault along the southern edge of the Malldraeth syncline and the Dinorwic fault flanking the Menai Straits, both of which have large down-throws to the north perhaps as a local feature of more extended tear faulting.

In broad regional distribution the Carboniferous Limestone in its peripheral outcrops about the Lower Palaeozoic rocks behaves as the flanking apron of a dome that formed the basic Hercynian structure of North Wales. The Vale of Clwyd then has the appearance of a downwarp on the north-eastern flank in which outliers of younger rocks—Upper Carboniferous and Triassic—are preserved. Its faulted margins show it to be a combined syncline and rift: and the fracturing of the New Red Sandstone proves that there was renewed movement in post-Triassic times. It was nevertheless established by the Hercynian movements, if not earlier, for the Trias in places oversteps folded Carboniferous rocks (preserved in the northern part of the vale to thicknesses of the order of 4,000 ft) almost onto Silurian (see Fig. 32).

The Hercynian faulting was accompanied, or was closely followed, by mineralization of many of the fault belts. Metallic ores occur abundantly along the eastern Carboniferous outcrop, particularly on Halkyn Mountain and in the neighbourhood of Minera. They are almost completely restricted to the Carboniferous Limestone and the overlying Cefn-y-fedw Sandstone, though only sparingly in the Basement Beds and in the Lower Grey and Brown Limestone. The chief minerals are zinc sulphide (blende) and lead sulphide (galena), with a little silver; with them are associated copper pyrites, barytes, and fluorspar. Ores also occur in the underlying Ordovician and Silurian rocks, but in quantity much less than in the Carboniferous; they are usually found in beds of fine sandstone and silt, lying between, or capped by, beds of shales.

The ores occur as thin ribs, developed along joints and faults that cut through the rock. Although no contemporaneous igneous activity is known in the neighbourhood, and although the development of minerals in the underlying Ordovician and Silurian rocks is relatively insignificant, it is probable that magmatic solutions from deep-seated sources carried the ores into the country rock in which they now occur, the solutions moving under pressure along the fractures, and depositing their metallic contents as they cooled and solidified. Apart from occurring along joints and faults (as east to west ' veins ' and north to south ' cross-courses '), the bodies of ore also follow bedding planes in the Limestone, where the calcite has been dissolved away to leave space for ' flats ' and ' runs ' of galena and blende. Beds of shale in the Limestone, more or less impervious to the upward-moving solutions, were important in determining deposition of ore, and the veins and flats tend to be richest beneath a cover of shale, or in the beds of pure limestone between shale bands.

The ore, so largely dependent in its distribution on the structural features, and upon the occurrence of lithologically suitable country rocks (especially of soluble limestone rocks), must have been introduced after the formation of the joints and faults, which are mainly of Hercynian age, but before deposition of the overlying Triassic sediments, for derived fragments of galena have been found in the New Red Sandstone of the neighbouring Shropshire–Cheshire Plain.

X. THE MESOZOIC ERA

Transgression of the New Red Sandstone

THE HERCYNIAN MOVEMENTS brought to a close the period of subsidence and deposition represented in the Upper Palaeozoic rocks, and at the end of Carboniferous times the whole of North Wales was uplifted to form part of a huge continent, a very much enlarged 'St. George's Land', the shores of which lay many miles to the south and east. Over this area an arid climate prevailed for a long interval, the deposits that rest on the Coal Measures being very different from the limestones, mudstones, and buff sandstones of the Carboniferous system. The environmental changes compare with the changes at the close of Lower Palaeozoic times, when the Caledonian earth-movements were the cause of the elevation of a continental landmass subjected to erosion in the semi-arid climate of Old Red Sandstone times. The analogy becomes even closer when the red sandstones, marls, and conglomerates of the New Red Sandstone are compared with those of the Old.

During the early part of the Mesozoic era a lake or inland sea existed on the northern and eastern flanks of North Wales in which Permian and Triassic deposits accumulated. As Mesozoic times advanced, the floor of the basin gradually subsided and the lake was extended by the progressive drowning of the marginal lowlands of the neighbouring landmass: by Triassic times subsidence had proceeded sufficiently to cause the submergence of the Flintshire and Denbighshire coalfields beneath waters that deepened eastwards over the present Shropshire–Cheshire Plain.

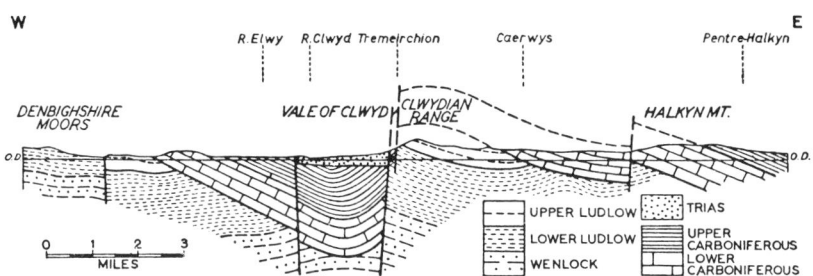

FIG. 32: *Section across the northern part of the Vale of Clwyd*

The vertical scale, and the dips in the Upper Palaezoic rocks, are exaggerated; and the structure of the Lower Palaeozoic rocks at depth is conjectural.

A depression also existed where now lies the Irish Sea, and a great embayment of the same basin lapped the western flanks of the hills of the Pennines and the hills of the North Wales massif. The Vale of Clwyd at this period had come into being as the result of rift faulting, and a gulf extended southwards from the basin to fill the Vale (see Fig. 32). To the west a similar basin in which New Red Sandstone was deposited occupied a trough where is now Cardigan Bay.

The period of Hercynian movement, when North Wales was elevated above levels of sedimentation, and the subsequent Permian period, when submergence had not as yet resulted in a burial of the area beneath younger deposits, were times of intense erosion; and the red beds of the Trias, which accumulated in the lake that finally transgressed on to the eastern and northern flanks of the area, are banked against and rest unconformably upon the worn-down edges of the Carboniferous rocks. North of Wrexham the Trias oversteps Coal Measures onto an upwarp of Millstone Grit; and along the southern part of their outcrop, in the neighbourhood of Oswestry and Llanymynech, the Trias oversteps the whole of the Carboniferous, and comes to rest on Lower Palaeozoic rocks. A similar structural relationship holds in the Vale of Clwyd, where the Trias rests in places upon Upper, in places upon Lower, Carboniferous rocks (see Fig. 26, p. 62).

In North Wales the New Red Sandstone is represented only by the Bunter sandstones and pebble-beds. They are soft rocks, mainly red in colour, but in places of variegated tints and mottlings, and generally so coarsely false-bedded as to make difficult measurements of their true dip. Locally beds of breccia and conglomerate occur, especially towards the base of the group. The general lithology suggests accumulation in shallow waters into which fluctuating and seasonal torrents from near-by land carried storm deposits that piled up as irregular and impersistent wedges and lenses near the confluences of rivers and lake. Many of the beds are of well rounded and sorted sand grains, and owe their origin to wind transport. Fossils are completely absent—an absence consonant with sedimentation in an inland basin under continental desert conditions.

Later Mesozoic Times

No Mesozoic rocks younger than the Bunter occur in North Wales, and the whole of the Jurassic and Cretaceous periods, together with the later part of the Triassic, are entirely unrepresented by sediments that would enable some estimate to be made of the topographical and geographical conditions existing in the area during the long interval of 100 million years. Only six miles from its eastern margin, however, in the low ground east of Oswestry, the Keuper rocks of the Trias attain a thickness of over 1,000 ft, and at Prees, fifteen miles away, these in turn are capped by Lias clays that bear no sign of having been deposited near a shore-line: the whole sequence clearly indicates a continuation of the subsidence demonstrated by the Bunter rocks. It is therefore highly probable that at one time there was a considerable thickness of Keuper and Liassic (and perhaps later Jurassic) sediments that continued westwards to overlap the Bunter of Flintshire and Denbighshire and to extend for some distance towards the heart of North Wales, burying in the process landscapes of prolonged subaerial denudation.

It would be idle further to speculate here upon the possibility of still younger strata of Mesozoic age having extended across the Trias and Lias to rest upon Carboniferous and older rocks. It is sufficient to mention the various theories concerning the transgression of the Upper Cretaceous sea. Greenly, on the evidence of erratics contained in the ice-transported drift of Anglesey, which on other grounds is known to have been carried from the north-east, suggested that a small synclinal outlier of Chalk, resting upon older Mesozoic strata, exists on the floor of the Irish Sea a few miles to the north-east of Anglesey. Elsewhere in Britain the Chalk and the underlying Greensand are strongly transgressive deposits, laid down in an extensive sea, and the presumption thus is that Upper Cretaceous rocks may have overstepped, and finally perhaps completely buried, the Palaeozoic cores of North Wales, much as the Trias oversteps the eastern ranges.

In a different approach, various workers, notably Ramsay, Lake, Jukes-Brown, and Strahan, have shown that if the base of the Chalk of the Chiltern escarpment were continued north-westward with its present inclination it would rise towards and over-top the summits of the present-day Welsh hills, and they have concluded that it is likely the whole area was drowned by the Cretaceous sea and was buried beneath a cover of Chalk—the absence from the present-day landscape of any persisting relics of the Chalk being ascribed to the intensity of post-Cretaceous erosion. In conformity with this inference it has been argued that most of the summit levels of the higher hills of North Wales are closely coincident with an imaginary gently warped surface that declines radially from a focus about Snowdonia, and that this surface may be identified with the sub-Cretaceous floor, initially planed as a marine bench by the transgressive Cretaceous sea, from which all Chalk sediments have long been stripped.

These speculations, based entirely on circumstantial evidence, cannot be accepted with any great degree of assurance. On the one hand, no material relics of a Cretaceous cover have as yet come to light: even tough cherts and flints, that elsewhere in Britain are persistent survivals of erosion of the Greensand and the Chalk, are completely absent from the Welsh uplands. And on the other hand, the evolution of the present-day Welsh landscape appears to have been much more complex than is expressed in the stripping and dissection of a sub-Cretaceous floor. While it is probable that the Chalk covered much of Wales, it is highly unlikely that any direct evidence of its having done so is still to be recognised.

At some time later than the Trias (perhaps following one of the uplifts that occurred before the beginning of the Eocene period) iron-bearing waters, percolating downwards, gave rise to the haematitic iron-ores, metasomatic replacements of Carboniferous Limestone, that are found in the Vale of Clwyd.

XI. THE TERTIARY ERA

VERY LITTLE is known of the sequence of events during Tertiary times—even less than of the events of Mesozoic times—for there are no deposits older than the Pleistocene glacial drifts to be found covering the Triassic and Palaeozoic rocks; and the total time gap unrepresented by sediments between Trias and Pleistocene is of the order of 180 million years. During much of the Tertiary era the contemporary seas of sedimentation were far to the south-east, where relics of large estuaries or deltas of rivers flowing from the west and north-west are preserved in the Eocene and Oligocene sands and clays of the London and Hampshire basins. North Wales was then above sea-level and undergoing intensive erosion, and the few indications that remain of the successive geographical changes it suffered must be read in the residual land forms of the present landscape.

During the mid-Tertiary Miocene earth-movements, ripples of the Alpine orogenic storm laid their impress strongly upon the Mesozoic and early Tertiary rocks of south and south-east England, and of South Wales, with the production of folds, faults, and overthrusts. It is probable that they also affected North Wales, as the post-Triassic folding and faulting in the Vale of Clwyd and in the lower Dee valley suggest: but in the Palaeozoic rocks the acute contortions and crumplings of the Caledonian movements, and the folding and fracturing of the Hercynian movements, shadow the later Miocene disturbances into insignificance, so that it becomes very difficult to separate the effects of the Tertiary orogeny from those produced in Palaeozoic times. Reiterating the earlier conception of a mid-Tertiary dome centred about Snowdonia, Lake has endeavoured to show that some of the faulting along the Bala line is of Tertiary age; and he similarly suggested that elsewhere Tertiary faulting, producing lines of weakness, is indicated by transverse river capture of radial streams of the original drainage of the uplifted domed surface. It is perhaps not without significance that these lines of faulting follow very closely the trend of the Caledonian folds and faults, and, if Lake's hypothesis is true, they provide good evidence of posthumous movement along ancient belts of disturbance.

PLATEAUS AND PLATFORMS

In regional development throughout Wales the dominant product of the long-continued erosion of Tertiary times is a gently undulating dissected plateau that in skyline profile transects indifferently rocks of all ages and the structures superimposed upon them (see Fig. 33). Its smooth and regular surface may have received its initial imprint during the transgression of the Mesozoic (notably the Cretaceous) seas; and in its basic form it may, as Ramsay first argued and Lake, Strahan, and O. T. Jones have agreed, be the product essentially of the simple exhumation of the sub-Mesozoic surface by progressive stripping of whatever Chalk and Jurassic rocks at one time formed the cover. But its dominant place in the landscape, and its well preserved smoothness over many hundreds of square miles, suggest a more recent finish to its form, the trenching of its surface by rivers and ice being then a comparatively late process not yet obliterating its main features.

78

Some indirect evidence of a maximum age for part of the plateau surface is provided by a small number of minor igneous intrusions, mainly occurring as doleritic dykes, that cut through the Lower Palaeozoic rocks and reach the surface chiefly in Anglesey and Lleyn but also in Snowdonia. Petrologically

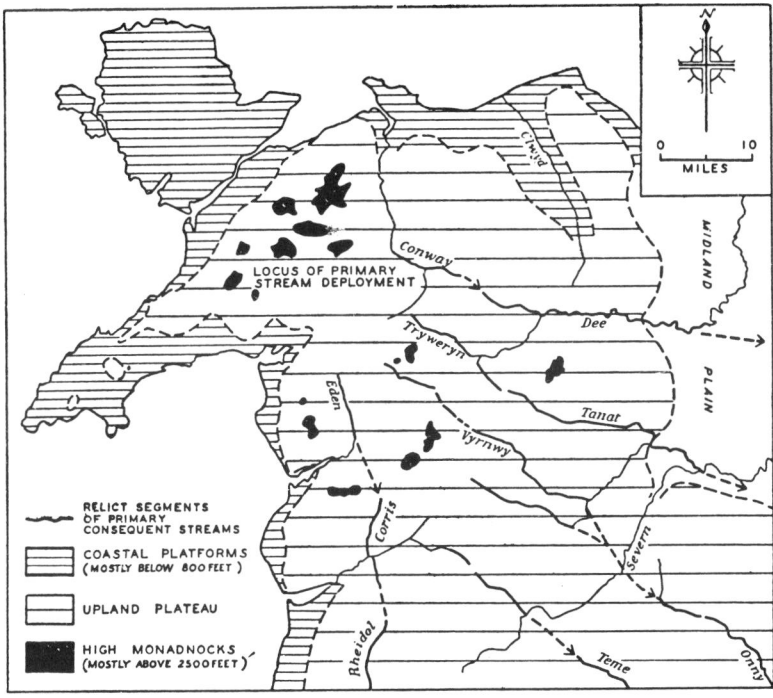

FIG. 33: *Map of the upland plateau and coastal platforms, and of the inferred primary drainage, of North Wales*
(In part after O. T. Jones and E. H. Brown.)

the dykes are composed of rock-types which, while falling into the same genus as the neighbouring Lower Palaeozoic dolerites, are relatively fresh and display closest affinity with rocks of the dyke-swarms of northern Britain, where Tertiary crustal unrest was marked by widespread vulcanicity rather than by folding: the dykes trend slightly west of north and may be regarded as offshoots comparable with the Cleveland dyke and the post-Triassic intrusions of the English Midlands. Since the dykes (at Marchllyn Mawr and Bwlch-y-Cywion, for instance) nowadays crop out at the height of the plateau, the plateau surface must obviously have been eroded at some time later than the period of intrusion, taken to be Eocene–Miocene.

In another method of analysis, Hollingworth has suggested that parts of the plateau reaching heights in north-central Wales of about 2,000 ft may not be significantly warped, since an equivalent platform at much the same height may be recognised in South Wales, the Lake District and the Southern Uplands. It is then to be regarded not as a remnant of a mid-Tertiary dome but as a bench bevelled (Brown surmised as a subaerial peneplain) across the flanks of any such dome which may have existed before its planation: above it the mountain peaks of Snowdonia, the Harlech country, Arenig and the Arans, Cader Idris, and the Berwyns now stand as residual monadnocks, whose summits may perhaps be the last relics of a sub-Mesozoic surface.

Subsequent to the Tertiary warping and the planation of the upland plateau, there was continued elevation of North Wales above sea-level. This elevation was intermittent, perhaps oscillatory (though the net effect was one of uplift); and during periods of quiescence or stillstand, when the relative levels of land and sea remained stationary, wave-cut platforms were eroded. These platforms nowadays fringe the coast at different levels, and provide evidence of the various positions of the shore-line during the later part of Tertiary times. As, however, the platforms carry no deposits, it is difficult to determine their precise age: in all probability they are Pliocene; certainly they, as well as most of the stream valleys cut into them, are pre-Pleistocene, for they underlie the drifts of the Ice Age (see Fig. 33).

The most spectacular of these platforms has been called by Greenly the Menaian Platform, of which the surface of Anglesey is the most extensive relic, though considerable tracts are also to be seen in Lleyn. It varies in height considerably and may be multiple: in places it is well below 200 ft, elsewhere it reaches nearly 300 ft: its average elevation is about 270 ft. It is incised by many rivers and waterways, the largest being the Menai Strait that separates Anglesey from the mainland; but these have not as yet greatly obscured its surface— indeed, as Ramsay remarked, no one looking to the north-east from the hills of the mainland of Caernarvonshire would suspect the existence of the Strait, so even and unbroken appears the surface of the platform. Where in places the land level descends to heights much below the average for the platform, isolated relict hills generally remain as ' islands ' in the plain to demonstrate its former extent, and bear witness to its subsequent erosion.

On the mainland of Caernarvonshire Dewey has recognised another shelf, a little over 400 ft above sea-level, that can be traced along the foot of the mountains of Snowdonia, from which it is suddenly and sharply demarcated by an abrupt change in slope and by a great contrast in topographical features. The mountains are rugged and precipitous, with bare rocky slopes devoid of vegetation. The upland plain is gently rolling, with smooth undulating curves breaking the horizontality of its surface, upon which vegetation is comparatively rich and agriculture flourishes. This platform, like the Menaian Platform, is attributed to marine planation: its abruptly defined cliffed margin, clearly discernible on the mainland, can perhaps also be recognized on the slopes of Mynydd Bodafon and Parys Mountain in Anglesey.

Yet a third platform is probably represented in the summits of the isolated relict hills (the ' monadnocks ') of Anglesey that project abruptly above the mean level of the Menaian Platform. These are Bwrdd Arthur, Llanddona Common, Mynydd Llwydiarth, Mynydd Bodafon, Nebo, Mynydd Eilian, and Mynydd-y-Garn, all of which are between 500 and 600 ft above sea-level. Greenly has called this the Monadnock Platform. A corresponding feature is widely developed in Lleyn (see Pl. VIIIB).

RIVER SYSTEMS

The principal rivers of North Wales follow courses that are unrelated to the geological structure, crossing indifferently folds, faults, and bands of hard and soft rocks. They thus appear to be superimposed and to have incised their valleys from a surface that may be deduced from the down-slope courses followed by the primary streams. The asymmetry of the main systems is clearly brought out by the concentration of headwaters in the north-western mountains, and by the contrast between the short steep profiles of most of the valleys draining into Cardigan and Caernarvon bays with the long gentle profiles of the valleys draining into England. So far as it can be reconstructed, the primary drainage plan appears to have been sub-radial, from a core or a ridge centred about Snowdonia, the radial spokes then suggesting a gently domed foundation land-form. This forms part of the argument for superimposition from a Cretaceous cover that Lake put forward; but the dome could as well be the result of up-warping of a peneplaned post-Cretaceous surface, and the rivers provide no clue to age (see Fig. 33).

The initial radial courses of the primary consequent streams were dis-membered by later capture and diversion by subsequent streams developing in adjustment to the geological structure. Thus the Upper Conway was probably at one time the source of the Dee, and the Dee itself a major tributary of the Trent; the Tryweryn fed the Tanat; and the Eden may have crossed the present line of the Wnion-Mawddach to run into the Dyfi. On such an interpretation of a reintegrated drainage, both the lower Conway and the Clwyd are secondary streams, the latter effective in piracy by following the outcrop of relatively soft Triassic rocks.

The influence of pulsatory uplift is discernible in the form of the major river valleys, which nearly all display deep incision beneath the surrounding plateau level: the Ogwen (Pl. X), the Conway, the Clwyd, the Dee, the Ceiriog, and the Vyrnwy are typical examples, even when the effects of glacial over-deepening are discounted. Successive stages in the episodic rejuvenation are indicated by the composite profiles of the valleys, which in longitudinal section display nick-points as cascades and waterfalls, and in transverse section terraces and benches. Although the pre-Glacial details have been mutilated or obscured by Pleistocene ice-erosion, Miller in the Dolgelley district and Embleton and others in north-east Wales have shown that former base-levels of erosion to which the rivers were graded—base-levels virtually equivalent to the contemporary sea-level of Cardigan Bay and the Irish Sea—lay progressively at heights of about 1,000 ft, 550 ft, 450 ft, and 200 ft above present-day sea-level. The last three agree well with the levels of the elevated marine platforms recognised in Caer-narvonshire and Anglesey.

XII. GLACIAL AND RECENT DEPOSITS

THE PROGRESSIVE deterioration of climate that is indicated in the Eocene, Oligocene, and Pliocene Tertiary sediments of the south and east of England reached its culmination in the onset of arctic conditions during the succeeding Pleistocene period. This, the Great Ice Age, was a time when the greater part of Britain was intermittently submerged beneath a blanket of ice that at its maximum attained a thickness of several thousand feet. Arctic conditions did not persist uninterruptedly throughout the whole of the Pleistocene, however, and the expansion of the snowcaps from the summits of the mountains, and the periodic advances of glaciers and ice-sheets, were broken by more genial interludes when climatic conditions were not unfavourable to the growth of plants, to the migration of many kinds of animals, and to the habitation of man. The Glacial Period was thus multiple, composed of a number of minor ice ages, of which four, or possibly five, have been recognised in northern Britain.

ICE-FLOWS

During the Pleistocene, mountainous North Wales was an area of considerable snowfall. The snow-caps were initially confined to the mountain summits, but with more intense cold glaciers began to form in the upland valleys and descended to lower and lower levels until, splaying out on the lowland plains, they coalesced to form continuous sheets of ice. From the major centres of dispersion the ice flowed in a general radial direction, eastwards to the Shropshire–Cheshire plain, northwards into the Irish Sea, westwards into Cardigan Bay and St. George's Channel. Within the main mountain area there were subsidiary loci of ice accumulation and deployment, of which the chief were, on the west, Snowdonia, the Harlech Dome, the Arans and the Cader Idris range, from which movement was principally towards the west and the north-west, and, on the east, the Arenigs and the Berwyns, material from which largely contributed to the moraines and outwash gravels of the Vale of Clwyd, the Dee and upper Severn valleys, and the Shropshire–Cheshire plain (see Fig. 34).

At times, as Greenly has shown, the mass of ice piling up in the heart of the mountains, as near Trawsfynydd, reached such dimensions that it behaved as a single unit and moved seawards with force sufficient to enable at least its upper layers to over-ride and striate even the eastern scarp face of parts of the Harlech Dome, some 2,000 ft above sea-level. It could then have been little less than 3,000 ft thick, so that many of even the larger hill masses offered only minor resistance to its direct course; and from the ice-shed between the Harlech Dome and the Arenigs an eastward movement, shouldered off by the Berwyns, carried Arenig boulders across Denbighshire out onto the Cheshire plain. Generally, however, especially when glaciation was less intense, the separate ranges or mountain groups behaved as distinct centres of restricted dispersion.

Contemporaneous with the glaciers of North Wales, ice flows from the Clyde valley and the Southern Uplands of Scotland, from the Lake District, and from the heights of north-eastern Ireland converged onto the depression of the Irish Sea. From this area of congestion the combined flows moved southwards under great pressure, part escaping directly into the Atlantic by St. George's Channel,

Plate IX

(A.6494)

A. The glaciated landscape of Llyn Llydaw

B. Llyn Cau

(A.6520)

but part being driven against the land mass of North Wales. This Irish Sea Ice, meeting the front of the Welsh mountains and the northward-flowing ice from Snowdonia and the Denbighshire uplands, split into two main streams in the

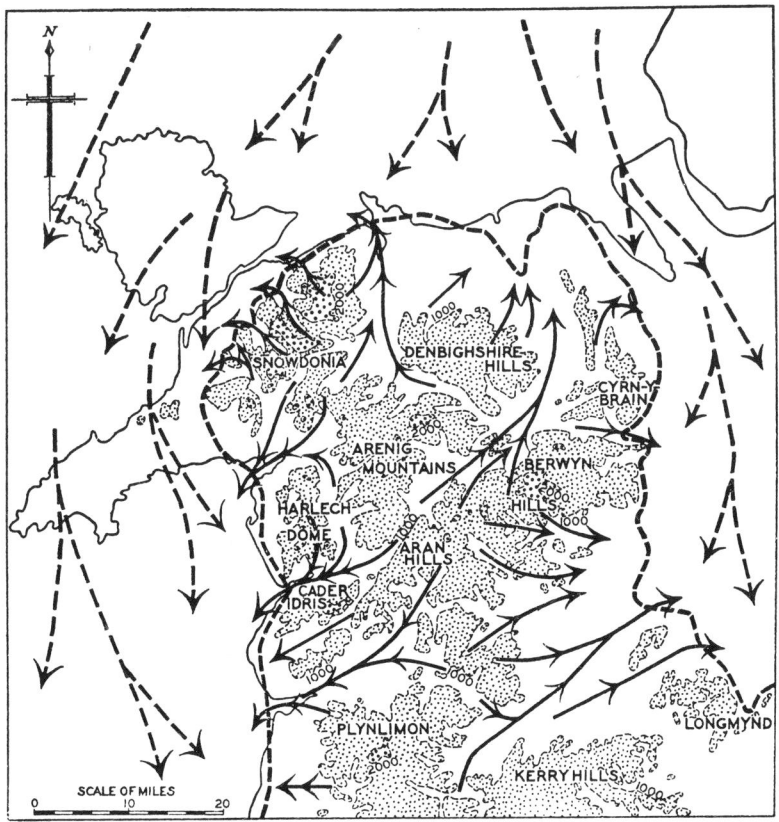

FIG. 34: *Map showing lines of ice-flow in North Wales*

The movements of Irish Sea ice, and the limits of its range, are shown by broken lines; the movements of local Welsh ice by continuous lines.

neighbourhood of the Great Orme: one branch was diverted south-westwards and flowed across Anglesey and the Menai region on to and across the Lleyn Peninsula into Cardigan Bay, the other branch moved south-eastwards and invaded the mouth of the Vale of Clwyd, the estuary of the Dee, and the Shropshire–Cheshire plain.

The extensions of the Irish Sea Ice upon the land surface, largely mapped by Strahan, Jehu, and Greenly, and by Survey officers on the eastern margin in recent years, are nowadays indicated by the occurrence of rocks derived from extra-Welsh sources. Thus Lake District rocks, including pebbles of Eskdale granite and Ennerdale granophyre, are common in the Drift deposits of Anglesey and Lleyn, of the northern coast, and of the Cheshire plain; while pebbles of the characteristic riebeckite-microgranite of Ailsa Craig (in the Firth of Clyde) and of the granites of Galloway have been found in Anglesey, on the mainland of Caernarvonshire, and in the lower Dee valley.

There also occur at various heights on the hill-slopes many patches of sand containing such marine shells as *Cyprina*, *Tellina*, *Turritella*, and *Cardium*, which were obviously dredged up from the sea-floor to the north and north-east, and were transported by the ice and deposited in their present positions on the mainland. Although the Irish Sea Ice was not able to override completely the mountains of North Wales, the great force of its movement may be gauged by the occurrence of patches of such ice-dredged marine sand at heights of nearly 1,400 ft on Moel Tryfaen between Caernarvon and Snowdon, of over 1,000 ft at Gloppa near Oswestry, and at various lower levels on the northern coast of Caernarvonshire, on Yr Eifl and other hills of Lleyn, and along the cliffs of the Harlech Dome between Harlech and Barmouth. The limits of the Irish Sea Drift, as thus determined by the distribution of erratics and marine sands, are delineated approximately on Fig. 34, while Fig. 35 shows the diversion of the Irish Sea Ice by the Welsh masses as illustrated by the distribution of boulder trains in Anglesey.

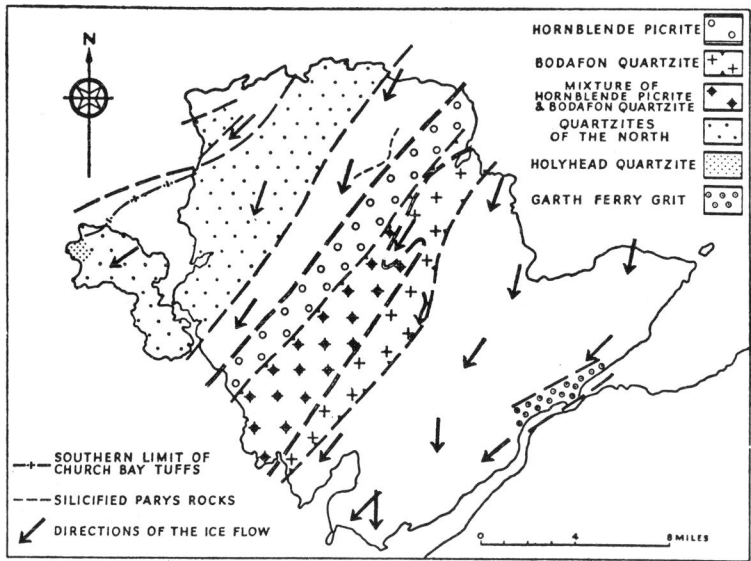

FIG. 35: *Trains of glacial erratics in Anglesey*
(After E. Greenly.)

The alignment of the trains is a sign of the direction of ice-transport. The arrows mark localities where direction is indicated by glacial striations or flutings.

Amongst the erratics from extra-Welsh sources in the glacial drift of Anglesey, Greenly found not only pebbles of Cretaceous flint but also fragments of iron-shot oolite similar to rock-types occurring commonly in the uppermost Liassic beds of England, together with faceted quartz pebbles and fragments of red sandstones and green marls with salt pseudomorphs that are unquestionably of Triassic age. Since the boulder-trains of Anglesey consistently show ice-flow from the north-east (Fig. 35), Greenly concluded that these erratics could have been dredged by the ice only from an extensive outcrop of Mesozoic rocks forming the floor of the Irish Sea east of a line joining Anglesey to the Isle of Man: the topographical depression of the sea floor is thus also the site of a geological downfold.

A. The Pass of Nant Ffrancon

(MN1913)

Plate X

B. The Pass of Nant Ffrancon during the Ice Age

(MN1912)

(A.6501)

A. Coast scenery and Yr Eifl near Nevin

Plate XI

B. The Mawddach estuary below Dolgelley

(A.6513)

The composite nature of the glaciation, made up of successive phases of advance and retreat of the ice, is not very clearly displayed in North Wales, and, partly because the glaciers repeatedly followed much the same courses and brought with them the same erratic rock types, it is difficult to distinguish one episode from the next. In Anglesey and Arvon, however, and along parts of the western border of the Cheshire plain, well-stratified fluviatile sands and gravels are intercalated between two layers of ice-deposited boulder clay, and it is to be concluded that there was at least one temporary amelioration of climate and a retreat of the ice (when the fluviatile beds were laid down) between two periods of glaciation.

The twofold origin of the ice affecting North Wales had marked effects on the river drainage that appeared in late-Glacial times. While the Irish Sea ice, fed from a number of sources and comparatively thick, still impinged on the Welsh coast, the ice-foot of local valley glaciers gradually migrated upstream with the onset of more genial conditions. The melt-waters of the glaciers in retreat thus met a barrier of stagnant Irish Sea ice along the coast, and were held up in temporary marjeelen lakes, the outflow of which followed devious channels over neighbouring cols. Similar phenomena on a smaller scale occurred when tributary streams entered glacier-occupied main valleys. Overflow channels formed under these conditions have been described by Greenly in Arvon, by Miller in the Barmouth estuary, and by Embleton in north-east Wales: and in the Lleyn peninsula Matley has described superficial deposits about Aberdaron, Abersoch, and Pwllheli that seem to be accumulations in an ice-dammed lake that spilled through a number of overflow channels cut in the adjacent hillsides.

GLACIAL EROSION

As Davis first clearly described, the subglacial rock surface, as now exposed to view after the melting of the ice, carries the scars of glacial erosion in a magnificent freshness that shows how recently—perhaps no more than 10,000 years ago—Wales ceased to have an arctic climate. Cirques, the chief feeding-grounds of mountain glaciers, abound in the Ordovician rocks around the Harlech Dome, and constitute a major element in the scenic grandeur of the Welsh mountains: the amphitheatre of Llyn Cau (Pl. IXB) on the southern flanks of Cader Idris is perhaps one of the most perfect cirque-forms in Britain. Although no true matterhorn peaks are to be found, the radial growth of cirques around Snowdon advanced so far as to leave little of the original smoothly rounded profile of the pre-Glacial mountains (Pl. VIIB). Many of the smaller lakes (Glaslyn, Llyn Idwal, Llyn-y-Gader, for instance) occupy cirque-hollows (Pl. I). The serrated arêtes and knife-edges, the widespread screes, the pinnacled crags are all related features. Most of the mountain glaciers were sufficiently powerful to over-deepen their containing valleys, which thus commonly have nearly vertical walls, bevelled spurs, and a characteristic U-shaped profile: the Llanberis (Pl. VIIA) and Nant Ffrancon passes, the Mawddach estuary below Dolgelley (Pl. XIB), the Dysinni valley about Talyllyn are examples: an attempt to illustrate conditions in the Nant Ffrancon valley during a late phase of the Ice Age is illustrated in Pl. X. In places the irregularly eroded valley floors have been hollowed into true rock basins and are now occupied by such elongate lakes as Llyn Peris and Llyn Padarn. Hanging valleys, with spectacular waterfalls like those at Bettws-y-Coed, are frequently developed where tributaries enter over-deepened main valleys.

GLACIAL DEPOSITS

On final waning at the close of the Glacial period, the ice left extensive swathings of drumlinoidal boulder clay, and eskers, deltas, and outwashes of sand and gravel, that overspread the wider valley bottoms and the low-lying coastal tracts and the Shropshire–Cheshire plain. Retreat stages in the melting of the valley glaciers are commonly marked by cross-moraines, sufficiently a barrier in many cases to hold up elongate valley lakes like Talyllyn, Llyn Tegid, Llyn Cwellyn, and the Mymbyr lakes. Many corries also have a morainic barrier rim holding back the corrie lake (see Pl. IX).

In the low ground the mounds of morainic boulder clay and gravels are very thick, and obliterated or greatly modified the pre-Glacial landscape (Pl. VIIIB). Post-Glacial streams initiated on the new surface when the ice finally melted follow courses that may then depart widely from the pre-Glacial pattern. A major instance is provided by the Dee. Evidence, gathered by L. J. Wills from deep borings that have penetrated the glacial drift to reach the 'solid' floor beneath, shows conclusively that the Dee originally flowed southwards from Cefn in the Vale of Llangollen through Chirk, thence swinging in a large half-circle around the hills of Ifton Heath, approximately through Ellesmere, to etch a persistent course near Bangor-on-Dee (Fig. 36 [1]). At that time it is probable that what is now the Upper Severn was a tributary of the Dee. At a number of localities the old valley floor of the Dee has been proved to lie many feet below present sea-level. On the final recession of the ice, the accumulation of drift on the flat ground near Chirk effectually obliterated the old valley (Fig. 36 [2]), and the river, swollen by water from the melting ice, overflowed directly eastwards, cutting a deep gorge towards Erbistock and Overton along which it has since continued to flow. The River Ceiriog was likewise compelled to adopt a new course, and overflowed north-eastwards to join the Dee above Erbistock; while the Severn, diverted southwards, was never able subsequently to break through the barrier of drift, and has since remained confluent with the River Stour.

BONE CAVES

In several districts in North Wales, particularly in the limestone tracts of the eastern hills, many caves hollowed out of the rocks by solvent ground water now contain highly fossiliferous deposits of cave earth of interglacial age. Those of the Vale of Clwyd (particularly the Prestatyn, Ffynnon Beuno, Cae Gwyn, and Llandegla caves) have long been famous. Often they contain relics of pre-historic animals, long extinct in Britain, while many of them also provide evidence of occupation by men of the Old Stone Age before the last advance of the ice buried the district under a more or less thick layer of glacial drift. Amongst the animals have been recognised lion, bear, hyaena, Irish deer, reindeer, woolly rhinoceros, and mammoth. Relics of human handiwork include flint knives and scrapers of types that elsewhere are often found associated with the skeletons of Aurignacian men.

POST-GLACIAL CHANGES

At the end of the Ice Age, North Wales was thus, not only in broad outline but also in very considerable detail, much as it is at present, and the principal changes that have occurred in post-Glacial times have been due to slight

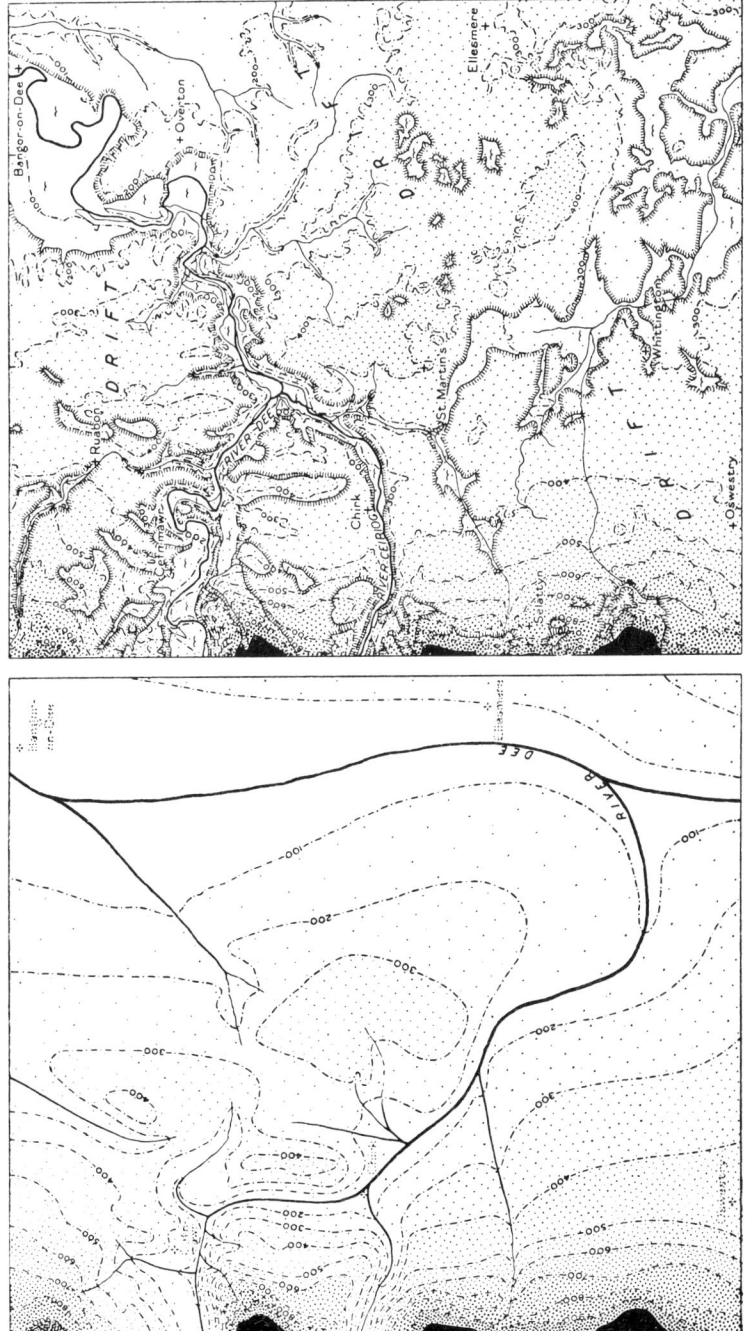

FIG. 36: *Maps showing diversions of the River Dee*

subsidence. Evidence of the subsidence is provided by the drowned valleys of
Cardigan Bay and the north coast—the estuaries of the Glaslyn river and the
Vale of Ffestiniog between Portmadoc and Harlech (the Deudraeth), the Dysinni
nèar Towyn, the Mawddach, the Dyfi, the Conway, and the Dee. In all these
cases the ' solid ' rock floor of the valleys is many feet below sea-level (at
Barmouth, for instance, it was proved in the foundations of the viaduct to be
more than 120 ft); and the valley mouths would be drowned, to appear very
like the fiords of Norway, if all the accumulations of alluvium and sand were
removed. No doubt the fiord-like form is in part the product of glacial over-
deepening (Pl. XIв), but it is also due to active depression of the land relative to
the sea—or conversely is due to rise in sea-level relative to the land—since at
many localities along the coast occur relics of submerged peats with plant
remains still in the position of growth. The peats, nowadays exposed at low-
water mark (and found in excavations at still lower levels), consist of masses of
humus with stumps and boles of such trees as oak, alder, hazel, pine, and birch
showing they must have accumulated at levels at least some feet above high-
water mark. At the same time, although the net effect of post-Glacial movement
is one of subsidence, gross movement was oscillatory; for interbedded with the
peats are marine and estuarine clays indicating some interruption to the
continuity of the gradual drowning. To this post-Glacial subsidence, as Greenly
has argued, may also be attributed the separation of Anglesey from the mainland
by the drowning of the watershed between two short valleys to form the Menai
Strait (which at the shallowest point is only 40 ft deep).

It is manifest also that there has been much modification of the superficial
geography of the coast-line by the silting up of the mouths of the drowned
estuaries, and by the growth and migration of sand dunes to form spits and bars
providing a protective barrier against the sea, behind which shallow but extensive accumulations of estuarine and alluvial muds and silts form ill-drained
marshy ground. The changes, which are still continuing, are strongly controlled
by the prevailing winds and currents. Beach material in Cardigan Bay is carried
dominantly northwards by long-shore drift, the tongues of beach gravel forming
a foundation for the wind-blown dunes, miles in length, of the Borth, Fairbourne, Dyffryn, and Harlech coasts; along the southern Lleyn coast growth
of the shingle ridges, not so spectacular, is eastwards. Tremadoc Bay is thus
progressively choked, and the Deudraeth is floored by a vast expanse of detritus
partly brought down as alluvium by the Glaslyn and Dwyryd rivers, partly
carried as shore sand into the estuary by flowing tides. On the north coast the
processes are well seen in the sand seas at the western end of the Menai Strait,
notably in Newborough Warren in Anglesey, in the barrier dunes at the mouth
of the Vale of Clwyd between Abergele and Prestatyn, and in the Point of Air.

The changes, involving transport of material from a variety of parent sources,
include a removal of some of the finer matrix from submarine morainic accumulations; and the residual glacial boulders, sometimes exposed by the ebbing
tide, may simulate the debris of artificial structures: Llys Helyg in Conway
Bay and Sarn Badrig in Cardigan Bay are such remnants of boulder-clay banks,
and are less romantic in origin than the walls and causeways of the drowned
lands and villages of early medieval Traeth Lafan and Cantref y Gwaelod.

XIII. BIBLIOGRAPHY

SOME OF THE MORE IMPORTANT PUBLICATIONS RELATING TO THE GEOLOGY OF NORTH WALES

Memoirs of the Geological Survey[1]

The geology of North Wales. 2nd Edition, 1881.

The geology of the country around Liverpool, with Wirral and part of the Flint-shire coalfield. (Sheet N.S. 96) 1923.

The geology of the country around Flint, Hawarden, and Caergwrle. (Sheet N.S. 108.) 1924.

The geology of the country around Wrexham. (Sheet N.S. 121) Part I. 1927. Part II. 1928.

The geology of the country around Oswestry. (Sheet N.S. 137) 1929.

The geology of the coasts adjoining Rhyl, Abergele, and Colwyn. (Sheet O.S. 79 N.W.) 1885.

The geology of the neighbourhoods of Flint, Mold, and Ruthin. (Sheet O.S. 79 S.E.) 1890.

The geology of Anglesey. 2 vols. 1919.

Special Reports on Mineral Resources[1]

    I. Tungsten and manganese. 3rd Edition. 1923.

    VI. Refractory materials. 2nd Edition. 1920.

    IX. Iron ores. 1919.

    XIII. Iron ores. 1920.

    XIV. Fireclays. 1920.

    XIX. Lead and zinc. 1921.

XXIII. Lead and zinc. 1922.

XXX. Copper ores. 1925.

Maps of the Geological Survey[1]

Quarter inch to 1 mile—Nos. 9 and 10. 1930.

1 inch to 1 mile:

New Series. Colour-printed

92 and 93.	Anglesey. Drift edition. 1920.			
96.	Liverpool. Solid and drift editions. 1923.			
108.	Flint.	,,	,,	,,	1924.
121.	Wrexham.	,,	,,	,,	1927.
137.	Oswestry.	,,	,,	,,	1928.

Old Series. Hand-coloured. Solid edition only

59. N.E.	Barmouth, Dolgelly. 1855.
59. S.E.	Machynlleth, Aberdovey. 1848.
60. N.W.	Dinas Mawddwy. 1855.
60. N.E.	Welshpool, part of Shropshire. 1855.
60. S.W.	Llanidloes. 1850.
60. S.E.	Montgomery, Newtown, part of Shropshire. 1850.
74. N.W.	Corwen. 1855.
74. S.W.	Bala. 1855.
75. N.W.	Nevin. 1850.
75. N.E.	Snowdon. 1854.
75. S.W.	Pwllheli, Criccieth. 1851.
75. S.E.	Harlech. 1855.

---

[1]Stocks of Geological Survey publications were destroyed by enemy action; reprinting of new series maps is in hand.

76. S.   South-western Lleyn. 1850.
78. N.E.   Anglesey, Conway. 1852.
78. S.W.   Anglesey, Caernarvon. 1852.
78. S.E.   Bangor, Llanberis, Bethesda. 1852.
79. S.W.   Vale of Clwyd, Denbigh. 1895.

Horizontal Sections of the Geological Survey

26. From Cardigan Bay across the Cader Idris range. 1880.
27. From the Menai Straits across Snowdon. 1880.
29. Across the Aran mountains. 1880.
31. From the Menai Straits across the Glyders and Moel Siabod. 1880.
32. Across the Bala country. 1880.
34. From near Welshpool into Shropshire. 1854.
35. Across the Berwyn Hills. 1853.
37. From the Harlech Dome across the Berwyn Hills to the Denbighshire coalfield. 1854.
38. From near Meifod across the Dee Valley to the Vale of Clwyd. 1855.
39. From Arenig Fawr to near Wrexham. 1880.
40. Across Anglesey. 1857.
43. From the Vale of Clwyd across the Clwydian Range and the Flintshire coalfield into Cheshire. 1892.
44. Across the Denbighshire coalfield. 1858.

Other Publications

General

1910. FEARNSIDES, W. G. The geology of North and Central Wales. In Geology in the Field. *Geol. Assoc.*, 786–824.
1956. JONES, O. T. The geological evolution of Wales and the adjoining regions. *Quart. Journ. Geol. Soc.*, vol. 111, pp. 323–51.
1928. NORTH, F. J. Geological maps. *Nat. Mus. Wales.*
1933. NORTH, F. J. From Giraldus Cambrensis to the geological map. *Trans. Cardiff Nat. Soc.*, vol. 64, pp. 20–97.
1934. NORTH, F. J. From the geological map to the Geological Survey. *Trans. Cardiff Nat. Soc.*, vol. 65, pp. 42–115.
1949. NORTH, F. J., B. CAMPBELL, and R. SCOTT. *Snowdonia*. London.

Structure

1958. BASSETT, D. A. Notes on the faults of the Bala district. *Liverpool & Manchester Geol. Journ.*, vol. 2, pp. 1–10.
1964. BLUNDELL, D. J., R. F. KING and C. D. V. WILSON. Seismic investigations of the rocks beneath the northern part of Cardigan Bay, Wales. *Quart. Journ. Geol. Soc.*, vol. 120, pp. 35–50.
1930. BOSWELL, P. G. H. The pre-Carboniferous history of the Vale of Clwyd. *Proc. Liverpool Geol. Soc.*, vol. 15, pp. 230–240.
1949. GREENLY, E. The cleavages of Mon and Arvon. *Proc. Liverpool Geol. Soc.*, vol. 20, pp. 23–37.
1961. GRIFFITHS, D. H., R. F. KING and C. D. V. WILSON. Geophysical investigations in Tremadoc Bay, North Wales. *Quart. Journ. Geol. Soc.*, vol. 117, pp. 171–91.
1950. JONES, O. T. The structural history of England and Wales. *Rep. 18th Int. Geol. Congr.*, vol. 1, pp. 216–29.
1955. JONES, O. T. The trends of geological structures in relation to directions of maximum compression. *Adv. Sci.*, vol. 11, pp. 102–6.
1956. POWELL, D. W. Gravity and magnetic anomalies in North Wales. *Quart. Journ. Geol. Soc.*, vol. 111, pp. 375–97.
1958. SHACKLETON, R. M. The structural evolution of North Wales. *Liverpool & Manchester Geol. Journ.*, vol. 1, pp. 261–96.
1965. SMITH, E. G., T. R. W. Hawkins, P. T. Warren and H. E. Wilson. A note on the pattern of faulting in the Ludlow rocks of north-western Denbighshire. *Bull. Geol. Surv. Gt. Brit.*, No. 23, pp. 1–8.
1899. STRAHAN, A. The age of the Vale of Clwyd. *Geol. Mag.*, vol. 36, pp. 111–17.
1957. WILSON, C. D. V. Seismic and gravity surveys in the Vale of Clwyd, North Wales. *Proc. Geol. Soc.*, no. 1543, pp. 10–11.

Pre-Cambrian

1954. BAILEY, E. B. The Mona Complex in Lleyn and its relation to the Ordovician. *Adv. Sci.*, vol. 11, p. 108.

1923. GREENLY, E. Further researches on the succession and metamorphism in the Mona Complex of Anglesey. *Quart. Journ. Geol. Soc.*, vol. 79, pp. 334–51.

1930. GREENLY, E. Foliation and its relation to folding in the Mona Complex at Rhoscolyn. *Quart. Journ. Geol. Soc.*, vol. 86, pp. 169–90.

1944. GREENLY, E. The Arvonian rocks of Arvon. *Quart. Journ. Geol. Soc.*, vol. 100, pp. 269–87.

1946. GREENLY, E. The geology of the city of Bangor. *Proc. Liverpool Geol. Soc.*, vol. 19, pp. 105–12.

1913. MATLEY, C. A. The geology of Bardsey Island. *Quart. Journ. Geol. Soc.*, vol. 69, pp. 514–33.

1928. MATLEY, C. A. The Pre-Cambrian complex and associated rocks of south-western Lleyn. *Quart. Journ. Geol. Soc.*, vol. 84, pp. 440–504.

1936. MATLEY, C. A., and B. SMITH. The age of the Sarn granite. *Quart. Journ. Geol. Soc.*, vol. 92, pp. 188–200.

1954. SHACKLETON, R. M. The structure and succession of Anglesey and the Lleyn peninsula. *Adv. Sci.*, vol. 11, pp. 106–8.

1956. SHACKLETON, R. M. Notes on the structure and relations of the Pre-Cambrian and Ordovician rocks of south-western Lleyn (Caernarvonshire). *Liverpool & Manchester Geol. Journ.*, vol. 1, pp. 400–9.

Lower Palaeozoic

1921. COX, A. H., and A. K. WELLS. The Lower Palaeozoic rocks of the Arthog-Dolgelley district. *Quart. Journ. Geol. Soc.*, vol. 76, pp. 254–324.

1927. COX, A. H., and A. K. WELLS. The geology of the Dolgelley district. *Proc. Geol. Assoc.*, vol. 38, pp. 265–318.

1909. ELLES, G. L. On the relation of the Ordovician and Silurian rocks of Conway. *Quart. Journ. Geol. Soc.*, vol. 65, pp. 169–92.

1943. FEARNSIDES, W. G., and W. DAVIES. The geology of Deudraeth: the country between Traeth Mawr and Traeth Bach, Merioneth. *Quart. Journ. Geol. Soc.*, vol. 99, pp. 247–76.

1963. GEORGE, T. N. Palaeozoic growth of the British Caledonides. In M. R. W. Johnson and F. H. Stewart (editors): *The British Caledonides*, 1–33. Edinburgh and London.

1908. GROOM, T. T., and P. LAKE. The Bala and Llandovery rocks of Glyn Ceiriog. *Quart. Journ. Geol. Soc.*, vol. 64, pp. 546–95.

1938. JONES, O. T. On the evolution of a geosyncline. *Quart. Journ. Geol. Soc.*, vol. 94, pp. lx–cx.

1916. JONES, O. T., and W. J. PUGH. The geology of the district around Machynlleth and the Llyfnant Valley. *Quart. Journ. Geol. Soc.*, vol. 71 (for 1915), pp. 343–85.

1839. MURCHISON, R. I. *The Silurian System*. London.

1946. NORTH, F. J. The slates of Wales. *Nat. Mus. Wales.*

1923. PUGH, W. J. The geology of the district around Corris and Aberllefenni. *Quart. Journ. Geol. Soc.*, vol. 79, pp. 508–41.

1928. PUGH, W. J. The geology of the district around Dinas Mawddwy. *Quart. Journ. Geol. Soc.*, vol. 84, pp. 345–81.

1929. PUGH, W. J. The geology of the district between Llanymawddwy and Llan-uwchllyn. *Quart. Journ. Geol. Soc.*, vol. 85, pp. 242–306.

1949. PUGH, W. J. Recent work on the Lower Palaeozoic rocks. *Adv. Sci.*, vol. 6, pp. 203–12.

1933. PULFREY, W. The iron-ore oolites and pisolites of North Wales. *Quart. Journ. Geol. Soc.*, vol. 89, pp. 401–30.

1853. RAMSAY, A. C. On the physical structure and succession of some of the Lower Palaeozoic rocks of North Wales and part of Shropshire. *Quart. Journ. Geol. Soc.*, vol. 9, pp. 161–79.

1843. SEDGWICK, A. Outline of the geological structure of North Wales. *Proc. Geol. Soc.*, vol. 4, pp. 212–24.

1844. SEDGWICK, A. On the older Palaeozoic rocks of North Wales. *Quart. Journ. Geol. Soc.*, vol. 1, pp. 5–20.

1855. SEDGWICK, A., and F. M‘COY. *A synopsis of the classification of the British Palaeozoic rocks, with a systematic description of the British Palaeozoic fossils.* London.

1844. SHARPE, D. Contributions to the geology of North Wales. *Quart. Journ. Geol. Soc.*, vol. 2, pp. 283–314.

1925. WELLS, A. K. The geology of the Rhobell Fawr district. *Quart. Journ. Geol. Soc.*, vol. 81, pp. 463–538.

1938. WHITTINGTON, H. B. The geology of the district around Llansantffraid-ym-Mechain, Montgomeryshire. *Quart. Journ. Geol. Soc.*, vol. 94, pp. 423–57.

1922. WILLS, L. J., and B. SMITH. The Lower Palaeozoic rocks of the Llangollen district. *Quart. Journ. Geol. Soc.*, vol. 78, pp. 176–226.

Cambrian

1910. ANDREW, A. R. The geology of the Dolgelley gold belt. *Geol. Mag.*, vol. 47, pp. 159–71, 201–11, 261–71.

1959. BASSETT, D. A., and E. K. WALTON. The Hell's Mouth Grits: Cambrian, greywackes in St. Tudwal's Peninsula, North Wales. *Quart. Journ. Geol. Soc.*, vol. 116, pp. 95–110.

1867–1869. BELT, T. On the ' Lingula Flags ' or ' Festiniog ' Group of the Dolgelly district. *Geol. Mag.*, vol. 4, pp. 493–5, 536–43; vol. 6, pp. 5–11.

1910. FEARNSIDES, W. G. The Tremadoc Slates and associated beds of south-east Carnarvonshire. *Quart. Journ. Geol. Soc.*, vol. 56, pp. 142–88.

1944. GREENLY, E. The Cambrian rocks of Arvon. *Geol. Mag.*, vol. 81, pp. 170–5.

1950. HOWELL, B. F., and C. J. STUBBLEFIELD. A revision of the fauna of the North Welsh *Conocoryphe viola* Beds implying a Lower Cambrian age. *Geol. Mag.*, vol. 87, pp. 1–16.

1959. KNILL, J. L. Axial and marginal sedimentation in geosynclinal basins. *Journ. Sed. Pet.*, vol. 29, pp. 317–25.

1954. KOPSTEIN, F. P. H. W. Graded bedding of the Harlech Dome. *Publ. Geol. Inst. R. Univ. Groningen*, 81.

1953. KUENEN, P. H. Graded bedding, with observations on Lower Palaeozoic rocks of Britain. *Verh. K. Ned. Akad. Wetensch.*, Afd. Natuurk. (1), vol. 20, no. 3.

1946. MATLEY, C. A., and T. S. WILSON. The Harlech Dome, north of the Barmouth estuary. *Quart. Journ. Geol. Soc.*, vol. 102, pp. 1–40.

1926. MORRIS, T. O., and W. G. FEARNSIDES. The stratigraphy and structure of the Cambrian slate-belt of Nantlle (Carmarthenshire). *Quart. Journ. Geol. Soc.*, vol. 82, pp. 250–303.

1915. NICHOLAS, T. C. The geology of St. Tudwal's Peninsula (Carnarvonshire). *Quart. Journ. Geol. Soc.*, vol. 71, pp. 83–143.

1916. NICHOLAS, T. C. Trilobite Fauna of the St. Tudwal's Peninsula. *Quart. Journ. Geol. Soc.*, vol. 71, pp. 451–72.

1956. STUBBLEFIELD, C. J. Cambrian palaeogeography in Britain. *In* Symposium sobre el Sistemo Cambrico, su Paleogeografia y el Problema de su Base, vol. 1, pp. 1–43. *Rep. XX Congr. Geol. Int.*

1938. WOODLAND, A. W. Petrological studies in the Harlech Grit Series of Merionethshire. *Geol. Mag.*, vol. 75, pp. 366–82, 440–54, 529–39.

1939. WOODLAND, A. W. The petrography and petrology of the Lower Cambrian manganese ore of west Merionethshire. *Quart. Journ. Geol. Soc.*, vol. 95, pp. 1–35.

1956. WOODLAND, A. W. The manganese deposits of Great Britain. *In* Symposium sobre yacimientos de manganeso, vol. 5, pp. 197–218. *Rep. XX Congr. Geol. Int.*

Ordovician

1963. BEAVON, R. V. The succession and structure east of the Glaslyn River, North Wales. *Quart. Journ. Geol. Soc.*, vol. 119, pp. 479–512.

1925. COX, A. H. The geology of the Cader Idris range. *Quart. Journ. Geol. Soc.*, vol. 81, pp. 539–94.

1936. DAVIES, D. A. B. The Ordovician rocks of the Trefriw district. *Quart. Journ. Geol. Soc.*, vol. 92, pp. 62–90.

1956. DAVIES, R. G. The Pen-y-gader dolerite and its metasomatic effects on the Llyn-y-gader sediments. *Geol. Mag.*, vol. 93, pp. 153–72.

1959. DAVIES, R. G. The Cader Idris granophyre and its associated rocks. *Quart. Journ. Geol. Soc.*, vol. 115, pp. 189–216.

1922. ELLES, G. L. The Bala country, its structure and rock succession. *Quart. Journ. Geol. Soc.*, vol. 78, pp. 132–72.

1905. FEARNSIDES, W. G. On the geology of Arenig Fawr and Moel Llyfnant. *Quart. Journ. Geol. Soc.*, vol. 61, pp. 608–40.

1944. GREENLY, E. The Ordovician rocks of Arvon. *Quart. Journ. Geol. Soc.*, vol. 100, pp. 75–83.

1950. GROVES, A. W. Results of a magnetometric survey of the Benallt mine, Rhiw, Caernarvonshire. *Trans. Inst. Min. Met.*, vol. 56, pp. 475–513.

1889. HARKER, A. *The Bala Volcanic Series of Caernarvonshire.* Cambridge.

1956. HARPER, J. C. The Ordovician succession near Llanystumdwy, Caernarvonshire. *Liverpool & Manchester Geol. Journ.*, vol. 1, pp. 385–93.

1926. JEHU, R. M. The geology of the district around Towyn and Abergynolwyn. *Quart. Journ. Geol. Soc.*, vol. 82, pp. 465–89.

1933. JONES, B. The geology of the Fairbourne–Llwyngwril district. *Quart. Journ. Geol. Soc.*, vol. 89, pp. 145–71.

1923. KING, W. B. R. The Upper Ordovician rocks of the south-western Berwyn Hills. *Quart. Journ. Geol. Soc.*, vol. 79, pp. 487–507.

1928. KING, W. B. R. The geology of the district around Meifod, Montgomeryshire. *Quart. Journ. Geol. Soc.*, vol. 84, pp. 671–702.

1926. LEWIS, H. P. On *Bolopora undosa* gen. et sp. nov.: a rock-building bryozoan with phosphatized skeleton from the basal Arenig rocks of Ffestiniog. *Quart. Journ. Geol. Soc.*, vol. 82, pp. 411–27.

1932. MATLEY, C. A. The geology of the country around Mynydd Rhiw and Sarn, south-western Lleyn *Quart. Journ. Geol. Soc.*, vol. 88, pp. 238–73.

1938. MATLEY, C. A. The geology of the country around Pwllheli, Llanbedrog, and Madryn (south-west Caernarvonshire). *Quart. Journ. Geol. Soc.*, vol. 94, pp. 555–606.

1930. MATLEY, C. A., and A. HEARD. The geology of the country around Bodfean. *Quart. Journ. Geol. Soc.*, vol. 86, pp. 130–68.

1958. RAST, N., R. V. BEAVON, and F. J. FITCH. Sub-aerial vulcanicity in Snowdonia. *Nature*, vol. 181, p. 508.

1961. RAST, N. Mid-Ordovician structures in south-western Snowdonia. *Liverpool and Manchester Geol. Journ.*, vol. 2, pp. 645–52.

1959. SHACKLETON, R. M. The stratigraphy of the Moel Hebog district between Snowdon and Tremadoc. *Liverpool & Manchester Geol. Journ.*, vol. 2, pp. 216–51.

1918. SHERLOCK, R. L. The geology and genesis of the Trefriw pyrites deposit. *Quart. Journ. Geol. Soc.*, vol. 74, pp. 106–15.

1935. SMITH, B. The Mynydd Cricor inlier. *Proc. Geol. Assoc.*, vol. 46, pp. 187–192.

1962. TREMLETT, W. E. The geology of the Nefyn-Llanaelhaiarn area of North Wales. *Liverpool and Manchester Geol. Journ.*, vol. 3, pp. 157–76.

1964. TREMLETT, W. E. The geology of the Clynnog-Fawr district and Gurn Ddu hills of northeast Lleyn. *Liverpool and Manchester Geol. Journ.*, vol. 4, pp. 207–23.

1955. WHITTINGTON, H. B., and A. WILLIAMS. The fauna of the Derfel Limestone of the Arenig district, North Wales. *Phil. Trans. Roy. Soc.*, B, vol. 238, pp. 397–427.

1930. WILLIAMS, D. The geology of the country between Nant Peris and Nant Ffrancon. *Quart. Journ. Geol. Soc.*, vol. 86, pp. 191–233.

1922. WILLIAMS, H. The igneous rocks of the Capel Curig district, *Proc. Liverpool Geol. Soc.*, vol. 13, pp. 166–202.

1927. WILLIAMS, H. The geology of Snowdon. *Quart. Journ. Geol. Soc.*, vol. 83, pp. 346–431.

1931. WILLIAMS, H., and O. M. B. BULMAN. The geology of the Dolwyddelan syncline. *Quart. Journ. Geol. Soc.*, vol. 87, pp. 425–58.

Silurian

1955. BASSETT, D. A. The Silurian rocks of the Talerddig district, Montgomeryshire. *Quart. Journ. Geol. Soc.*, vol. 111, pp. 239–64.

1928. BLACKIE, R. C. The geology of the country between Llanelidan and Bryneglwys. *Quart. Journ. Geol. Soc.*, vol. 83, pp. 711–35.

1926. BOSWELL, P. G. H. The geology of the eastern part of the Denbighshire Moors. *Quart. Journ. Geol. Soc.*, vol. 82, pp. 556–85.

1928. BOSWELL, P. G. H. The Salopian rocks and tectonics of the district south-west of Ruthin (Denbighshire). *Quart. Journ. Geol. Soc.*, vol. 83, pp. 689–710.

1928. BOSWELL, P. G. H. The cleavage-fan in the Silurian rocks of the Denbighshire Moors and Clwydian Range. *Proc. Liverpool Geol. Soc.*, vol. 15, pp. 69–77.

1931. BOSWELL, P. G. H. The Ludlow rocks of the northern part of the Clwydian Range. *Proc. Liverpool Geol. Soc.*, vol. 15, pp. 297–308.

1935. BOSWELL, P. G. H. The geology of north-western Denbighshire. *Proc. Geol. Assoc.*, vol. 46, pp. 152–86.

1937. BOSWELL, P. G. H. The tectonic problems of an area of Salopian rocks in north-western Denbighshire. *Quart. Journ. Geol. Soc.*, vol. 93, pp. 284–321.

1942. BOSWELL, P. G. H. The Wenlock and Ludlow rocks of the district around Gwytherin, north-western Denbighshire. *Proc. Liverpool Geol. Soc.*, vol. 18, pp. 86–100.

1943. BOSWELL, P. G. H. A revision of the geology of the area around Llyn-Goronwy, Llanrwst, Denbighshire. *Proc. Liverpool Geol. Soc.*, vol. 18, pp. 144–8.

1943. BOSWELL, P. G. H. The Salopian rocks and geological structure of the country around Eglwys-fach and Glan Conway, N.W. Denbighshire. *Proc. Geol. Assoc.*, vol. 54, pp. 93–112.

1949. BOSWELL, P. G. H. *The Middle Silurian rocks of North Wales*. London.

1953. BOSWELL, P. G. H. The alleged subaqueous sliding of large sheets of sediment in the Silurian rocks of North Wales. *Liverpool & Manchester Geol. Journ.*, vol. 1, pp. 148–52.

1934. BOSWELL, P. G. H., and I. S. DOUBLE. The Ludlow rocks of the northern part of the Denbigh Moors between Abergele and Llanfair-Talhaiarn. *Proc. Liverpool Geol. Soc.*, vol. xvi, pp. 156–72.

1938. BOSWELL, P. G. H., and I. S. DOUBLE. The Ludlow rocks and structure of the country in the neighbourhood of Llanfair-Talhaiarn and Llansannan, Denbighshire. *Proc. Liverpool Geol. Soc.*, vol. 17, pp. 277–311.

1940. BOSWELL, P. G. H., and I. S. DOUBLE. The geology of an area of Salopian rocks west [east] of the Conway valley, in the neighbourhood of Llanrwst, Denbighshire. *Proc. Geol. Assoc.*, vol. 51, pp. 151–87.

1957. CUMMINS, W. A. The Denbigh Grits: Wenlock greywackes in Wales. *Geol. Mag.*, vol. 44, pp. 433–51.

1959. CUMMINS, W. A. The Nantglyn Flags: mid-Salopian basin facies in Wales. *Liverpool & Manchester Geol. Journ.*, vol. 2, pp. 159–67.

1959. CUMMINS, W. A. The Lower Ludlow Grits in Wales. *Liverpool & Manchester Geol. Journ.*, vol. 2, pp. 168–79.

1896. ELLES, G. L., and E. M. R. WOOD. On the Llandovery and associated rocks of Conway (North Wales). *Quart. Journ. Geol. Soc.*, vol. 52, pp. 273–88.

1893. GROOM, T. T., and P. LAKE. On the Llandovery and associated rocks in the neighbourhood of Corwen. *Quart. Journ. Geol. Soc.*, vol. 49, pp. 426–40.

1937. JONES, O. T. On the sliding and slumping of submarine sediments in Denbighshire, North Wales, during the Ludlow period. *Quart. Journ. Geol. Soc.*, vol. 93, pp. 241–83.

1940. JONES, O. T. The geology of the Colwyn Bay district. *Quart. Journ. Geol. Soc.*, vol. 95, pp. 335–82.

1953. JONES, O. T. The use of graptolites in geological mapping. *Liverpool & Manchester Geol. Journ.*, vol. 1, pp. 246–60.

1895. LAKE, P. On the Denbighshire Series of south Denbighshire. *Quart. Journ. Geol. Soc.*, vol. 51, pp. 9–22.

1940. SIMPSON, B. The Salopian rocks of the Clwydian Range between the Bodfari gap and Moel Llys-y-Coed, Flintshire. *Proc. Geol. Assoc.*, vol. 51, pp. 188–206.

1911. WADE, A. On the Llandovery and associated rocks of north-east Montgomeryshire. *Quart. Journ. Geol. Soc.*, vol. 67, pp. 415–59.

1925. Woods, E. G., and M. C. Crosfield. The Silurian rocks of the central part of the Clwydian Range. *Quart. Journ. Geol. Soc.*, vol. 81, pp. 170–92.

Carboniferous

1958. George, T. N. Lower Carboniferous palaeogeography of the British Isles. *Proc. Yorks. Geol. Soc.*, vol. 31, pp. 227–318.

1928. Greenly, E. The Lower Carboniferous rocks of the Menaian region of Caernarvonshire. *Quart. Journ. Geol. Soc.*, vol. 84, pp. 382–439.

1906. Hind, W., and J. T. Stobbs. The Carboniferous succession below the Coal. Measures. *Geol. Mag.*, vol. 43, pp. 385–400, 445–59, 496–507.

1921. Jones, T. A. A contribution to the microscopic study of the Carboniferous Limestone of North Wales. *Proc. Liverpool Geol. Soc.*, vol. 13, pp. 78–99.

1940. Khosrovani, K. The correlation of strata at Halkyn mines, North Wales, by the study of insoluble residues. *Trans. Inst. Min. Met.*, vol. 49, pp. 473–511.

1930. Lloyd, W., and R. C. B. Jones. The Upper Carboniferous of Flintshire. *Geol. Mag.*, vol. 67, pp. 45–6.

1960. Magraw, D. and M. A. Calver. Faunal marker horizons in the middle Coal Measures of the North Wales Coalfield. *Proc. Yorks. Geol. Soc.*, vol. 32, pp. 333–52.

1878. Morton, G. H. The Carboniferous Limestone and Millstone Grit in the country around Llangollen. *Proc. Liverpool Geol. Soc.*, vol. 3, pp. 152–65, 299–325, 371–428.

1886. Morton, G. H. The Carboniferous Limestone and Cefn-y-fedw Sandstone of Flintshire. *Proc. Liverpool Geol. Soc.*, vol. 4, pp. 297–320, 381–403.

1897. Morton, G. H. The Carboniferous Limestone of the Vale of Clwyd. *Proc. Liverpool Geol. Soc.*, vol. 8, pp. 32–65, 181–204.

1898. Morton, G. H. The Carboniferous Limestone of the country around Llandudno. *Quart. Journ. Geol. Soc.*, vol. 54, pp. 382–400.

1929. Neaverson, E. Faunal horizons in the Carboniferous Limestone of the Vale of Clwyd. *Proc. Liverpool Geol. Soc.*, vol. 15, pp. 111–133.

1930. Neaverson, E. The Carboniferous rocks around Prestatyn, Dyserth, and Newmarket. *Proc. Liverpool Geol. Soc.*, vol. 15, pp. 179–212.

1937. Neaverson, E. The Carboniferous rocks between Llandudno and Colwyn Bay. *Proc. Liverpool Geol. Soc.*, vol. 17, pp. 115–135.

1945. Neaverson, E. The Carboniferous rocks between Abergele and Denbigh. *Proc. Liverpool Geol. Soc.*, vol. 19, pp. 52–68.

1946. Neaverson, E. The Carboniferous Limestone Series of North Wales: conditions of deposition and interpretation of its history. *Proc. Liverpool Geol. Soc.*, vol. 19, pp. 113–44.

1930. North, F. J. Coal and the coalfields of Wales. 2nd Edition. *Nat. Mus. Wales.*

1923. Sargent, H. C. The Massive Chert Formation of North Flintshire. *Geol. Mag.*, vol. 60, pp. 168–83.

1927. Sargent, H. C. The stratigraphical horizon and field relations of the Holywell Shales and ' Black Limestone ' of North Flintshire. *Geol. Mag.*, vol. 64, pp. 252–63.

1939. Schnellmann, G. A. Applied geology at Halkyn District United Mines. *Trans. Inst. Min. Met.*, vol. 48, pp. 585–650.

1959. Schnellmann, G. A. Lead-zinc mining in the Carboniferous Limestone of North Wales. *In symposium:* The Future of Non-Ferrous Mining in Great Britain and Ireland. *Inst. Min. Met.* London.

1956. Shanklin, J. K. New record of the *Gastrioceras listeri* Marine Band in Flintshire. *Liverpool and Manchester Geol. Journ.*, vol. 1, pp. 536–42.

1925. Smyth, L. B. A contribution to the geology of Great Orme's Head. *Proc. Roy. Dublin Soc.*, vol. 18, pp. 141–64.

1879. Strahan, A., and A. O. Walker. On the occurrence of pebbles with Upper Ludlow fossils in the Lower Carboniferous conglomerates of North Wales. *Quart. Journ. Geol. Soc.*, vol. 35, pp. 268–74.

1926. Walton, J. Contributions to the knowledge of Lower Carboniferous plants. *Phil. Trans. Roy. Soc.*, Ser. B, vol. 211, pp. 201–24.

1936. Wood, A. Goniatite zones in the Millstone Grit Series of North Wales. *Proc. Liverpool Geol. Soc.*, vol. 17, pp. 10–28.

1937. WOOD, A. The non-marine lamellibranchs of the North Wales Coalfield. *Quart. Journ. Geol. Soc.*, vol. 93, pp. 1–22.

Geomorphology

1956. BROWN, E. H. The 600-foot platform in Wales. *Proc. 17th Int. Geogr. Congr.*, pp. 304–12.

1957. BROWN, E. H. The physique of Wales. *Geog. Journ.*, vol. 123, pp. 208–30.

1960. BROWN, E. H. *The relief and drainage of Wales.* Cardiff.

1918. DEWEY, H. On the origin of some land forms in Caernarvonshire. *Geol. Mag.*, vol. 55, pp. 145–157.

1957. EMBLETON, C. Some stages in the drainage evolution of north-east Wales. *Trans. Inst. Brit. Geog.*, vol. 17, pp. 19–35.

1964. EMBLETON, C. The planation surfaces of Arfon and adjacent parts of Anglesey: a re-examination of their age and origin. *Trans. Inst. Brit. Geogr.*, vol. 35, pp. 17–26.

1961. GEORGE, T. N. The Welsh landscape. *Sci. Progr.*, vol. 49, pp. 242–64.

1938. GREENLY, E. The age of the mountains of Snowdonia. *Quart. Journ. Geol. Soc.*, vol. 94, pp. 117–24.

1920. GREGORY, J. W. The pre-Glacial valleys of Arran and Snowdon. *Geol. Mag.*, vol. 57, pp. 148–64.

1938. HOLLINGWORTH, S. E. The recognition and correlation of high-level erosion surfaces in Britain. *Quart. Journ. Geol. Soc.*, vol. 94, pp. 55–84.

1952. JONES, O. T. The drainage system of Wales and the adjacent regions. *Quart. Journ. Geol. Soc.*, vol. 107, pp. 201–25.

1900. LAKE, P. Bala Lake and the river system of North Wales. *Geol. Mag.*, vol. 37, pp. 204–15, 240–5.

1934. LAKE, P. The rivers of Wales and their connection with the Thames. *Science Progress*, No. 113, pp. 23–40.

1951. LINTON, D. L. Midland drainage: some considerations bearing on its origin. *Adv. Sci.*, vol. 7, pp. 449–56.

1939. MILLER, A. A. Pre-Glacial erosion surfaces around the Irish Sea basin. *Proc. Yorks. Geol. Soc.*, vol. 24, pp. 31–59.

1946. MILLER, A. A. Some physical features related to the river development in the Dolgelley district. *Proc. Geol. Assoc.*, vol. 57, pp. 174–203.

1946. STEERS, J. A. *The coastline of England and Wales.* Cambridge.

1956. WILKINSON, H. R., and S. GREGORY. Aspects of the evolution of the drainage-pattern of north-east Wales: the evidence of upper erosion surfaces. *Liverpool & Manchester Geol. Journ.*, vol. 1, pp. 543–57.

Pleistocene and Recent

1909. DAVIS, W. M. Glacial erosion in North Wales. *Quart. Journ. Geol. Soc.*, vol. 65, pp. 281–350.

1957. EMBLETON, C. Late-Glacial drainage in part of north-east Wales. *Proc. Geol. Assoc.*, vol. 67, pp. 393–404.

1961. EMBLETON, C. The geomorphology of the Vale of Conway, North Wales, with particular reference to its deglaciation. *Trans. Inst. Brit. Geogr.*, vol. 29, pp. 47–70.

1940. GODWIN, H. Pollen analysis and forest history of England and Wales. *New Phyt.*, vol. 39, pp. 370–400.

1942. GREENLY, E. Notes on the glacial phenomena of Arvon. *Quart. Journ. Geol. Soc.*, vol. 97, pp. 163–78.

1902. JEHU, T. J. Bathymetrical survey of the lakes of Snowdonia. *Trans. Roy. Soc. Edin.*, vol. 40, pp. 419–67.

1909. JEHU, T. J. The glacial deposits of western Caernarvonshire. *Trans. Roy. Soc. Edin.*, vol. 47, pp. 17–56.

1936. MATLEY, C. A. A 50-foot coastal terrace and other late-Glacial phenomena in the Lleyn peninsula. *Proc. Geol. Assoc.*, vol. 47, pp. 221–33.

1961. PEAKE, D. S. Glacial changes in the Alyn river system, and their significance in the glaciology of the North Welsh border. *Quart. Journ. Geol. Soc.*, vol. 117, pp. 335–66.

1860. RAMSAY, A. C. *The Old Glaciers of Switzerland and North Wales*. London.
1886. STRAHAN, A. On the glaciation of South Lancashire, Cheshire, and the Welsh border. *Quart. Journ. Geol. Soc.*, vol. 42, pp. 369–91.
1939. STEERS, J. A. Sand and shingle formations in Cardigan Bay. *Geog. Journ.*, vol. 44, pp. 209–27.
1964. SYNGE, F. M. The Glacial succession in west Caernarvonshire. *Proc. Geol. Assoc.*, vol. 75, pp. 431–44.
1944. TRAVIS, C. B. The glacial history of the Berwyn Hills. *Proc. Liverpool Geol. Soc.*, vol. 19, pp. 14–28.
1912. WILLS, L. J. Late-Glacial and post-Glacial changes in the lower Dee Valley. *Quart. Journ. Geol. Soc.*, vol. 58, pp. 180–98.

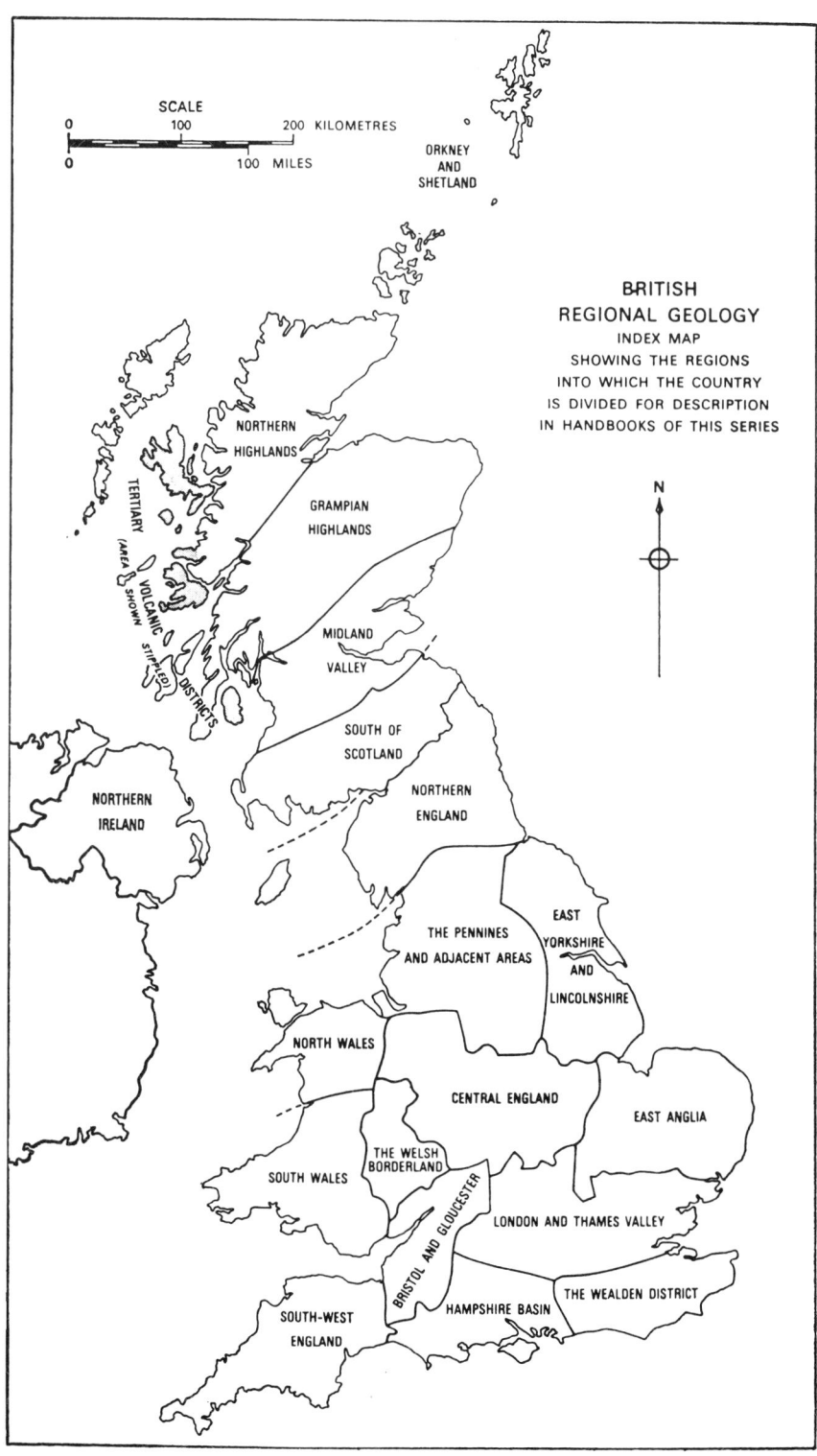

SCALE

0   100   200 KILOMETRES

0   100 MILES

ORKNEY
AND
SHETLAND

BRITISH
REGIONAL GEOLOGY
INDEX MAP
SHOWING THE REGIONS
INTO WHICH THE COUNTRY
IS DIVIDED FOR DESCRIPTION
IN HANDBOOKS OF THIS SERIES

N

NORTHERN
HIGHLANDS

TERTIARY (AREA VOLCANIC SHOWN STIPPLED) DISTRICTS

GRAMPIAN
HIGHLANDS

MIDLAND
VALLEY

SOUTH OF
SCOTLAND

NORTHERN
IRELAND

NORTHERN
ENGLAND

THE PENNINES
AND ADJACENT AREAS

EAST
YORKSHIRE
AND
LINCOLNSHIRE

NORTH WALES

CENTRAL ENGLAND

EAST ANGLIA

THE WELSH
BORDERLAND

SOUTH WALES

BRISTOL AND GLOUCESTER

LONDON AND THAMES VALLEY

SOUTH-WEST
ENGLAND

HAMPSHIRE BASIN

THE WEALDEN DISTRICT

Printed in the United Kingdom for Her Majesty's Stationery Office
Dd.238947/8.87/C50/3933/12521